Samuel James Watson

The Powers of Canadian Parliaments

Samuel James Watson

The Powers of Canadian Parliaments

ISBN/EAN: 9783337028596

Printed in Europe, USA, Canada, Australia, Japan

Cover: Foto ©Suzi / pixelio.de

More available books at **www.hansebooks.com**

THE POWERS

OF

CANADIAN PARLIAMENTS.

BY

S. J. WATSON,

Librarian of the Parliament of Ontario.

TORONTO:
C. B. ROBINSON, PRINTER, 5 JORDAN STREET.
1880.

INDEX.

CHAPTER I.

                                                                                           PAGE

"Parliament:" Use of the word, by Lieut.-Governor Gore; by Sir P. Maitland; by the Earl of Elgin; in the Confederation Resolutions; in the summoning of the Ontario and Quebec Houses . . . 9–10–11

Earl Carnarvon styles the "Legislature of the Dominion" the "Local Legislature" 11

CHAPTER II.

Lieut.-Governor Simcoe's address to the first Parliament of Upper Canada 12
His promise to the Speaker 12
Functions of the Parliament of Upper Canada 13
First use of the words, "Peace, Welfare and Good Government" . . 14
Mr. A. McDonnell pleads privilege against arrest 14–15
Dismissal of Mr. Baldwin, an officer of the Legislative Council, for his action *in re* McDonnell 15
Arrest of Mr. Nichol for breach of privilege 15–16
Speaker's warrant committing Mr. Nichol 17
Liberation of Mr. Nichol by Chief Justice Scott 17
Motion of the House that Chief Justice Scott has been guilty of a violent breach of privilege 17
Legislative Council disclaim right to interfere with Chief Justice Scott 18
He explains the reason why he liberated Nichol 17–20
The Assembly addresses the Prince Regent against the Chief Justice . 21

CHAPTER III.

The case of Messrs. Coffin and Givens; they refuse to attend a Committee; they are arrested and placed at the Bar of the House . . . 23
Their plea; they are committed on the Speaker's warrant 24
Message from Sir P. Maitland respecting these arrests 25–26
The case of Mr. Allan MacNab, a member of the House; his arrest for contempt and breach of privilege 27
Committed on the Speaker's warrant; discharged on his warrant . 27–28

	PAGE
MacNab v. Bidwell, and Baldwin in the King's Bench	28
Remarks of Chief Justice Robinson, in dismissing the case	28-30
Case of Solicitor-General Boulton, for contempt and breach of privilege	30
He is admonished and discharged by Mr. Speaker Bidwell	30-31

CHAPTER IV.

Committee of Public Accounts in the Assembly of Upper Canada, in 1812 32
Committee of Public Accounts in the Imperial House of Commons, half a century later. 32-23

CHAPTER V.

Privilege in Lower Canada; Mr. Young, a member of the Assembly, complains of breach of privilege in his arrest 33-34
Action of the House in the matter 34
The Speaker of the House apologises for acting as an advocate in the arrest of Mr. Young. 35
The House orders the arrest of the plaintiff *in re* Mr. Young 36
The Sheriff compelled to appear at the Bar and apologise for the arrest 36
Privilege pleaded against Jury Service 36-37
The House expels a Member for having been found guilty in the King's Bench of conspiracy to obtain money 38
The House commits one of the Prothonotaries of Montreal for refusing to produce certain records 38
He is discharged on account of the prorogation of the House 39
The House commits one Lacroix for false evidence 39
Privilege of the Legislative Council of Lower Canada; commitment of Tracy and Duvernay for libel 39-40
The case before the Courts; remarks of Mr. Justice Kerr 40-41
Remarks of Mr. Justice Bowen. 41-44

CHAPTER VI.

Privilege in the late Province of Canada 44
Commitment of Lebel, *in re* the Argenteuil Election, for breach of privilege 44
Mr. Brodeur, a Member, placed at the Bar for refusing to be examined as Returning Officer 45
Mr. Gleason placed at the Bar for sending a challenge to a Member . 45
Commitment of McCullough and Coté for breach of privilege *in re* the Lotbinière Election, 1858 45

	PAGE
Commitment of McCarthy, Guay, Lavoie and Tremblay for breach of privilege *in re* the Saguenay Election	45–46
Liberation of Lavoie; reasons therefor	46–47

CHAPTER VII.

Federal and Provincial powers compared	47–51
The Federal Parliament the offspring of the Provincial Legislatures	51
The reserved powers of the Provinces	52
French Jurisprudence in Quebec	52
Court of Divorce and Matrimonial Causes in New Brunswick	52
Power of the Provinces to amend their Constitutions; this power denied to the Federal Parliament	52
Right Hon. W. E. Gladstone on self-government in the Colonies	53
The Colonies, if they desire it, could have the appointment of their own Governors	53

CHAPTER VIII.

Sir John A. Macdonald's original memorandum on Disallowance of Provincial Acts	54–56

CHAPTER IX.

Privileges of the Ontario Legislature; Disallowance of the Act defining them	57
Sir John A. McDonald's report on this Act, 32 Vic., chap. 3	57–59
Hon. John Sandfield Macdonald's defence of the Act; his reply to Sir John A. Macdonald	59–65
Hon. John Sandfield Macdonald will not yield; submits no motion for the repeal of the Act	65
Disallowance of the Act	66

CHAPTER X.

Privileges of the Legislature of Quebec, 32 Vic., cap. 4; disallowance thereof	66
The Quebec Parliament passes another Act, 33 Vic., cap. 5	67
Summary of the Act	67
Difference between the Quebec Act and the Ontario Act, 39 Vic., cap. 9	67–68
Quebec Act allowed to go into operation	68

CHAPTER XI.

	PAGE
The Legislature of Ontario again asserts its privileges, 39 Vic., cap. 9 .	68
The powers devolving on the Parliament of Ontario by virtue of this Act; analysis of these powers	68-71

CHAPTER XII.

Ontario interferes in Federal Legislation	72
The breach of the terms of Confederation *in re* Nova Scotia subsidy	72
Hon. Mr. Blake's motion on the subject . . . . , . .	72
Resolution of the Legislature of Ontario	72

CHAPTER XIII.

The Quebec Judiciary pronounces on Provincial privileges	73
Case of Mr. Dansereau, 1875	73
The ruling of the Court	74
Mr. Justice Ramsay's condemnation of general warrants	74-75
Mr. Justice Sanborn's remarks	75
He shows how the British North America Act was enacted	75
"The late Province of Lower Canada has never lost its identity" . .	75
"No powers that have been conceded were intended to be taken away by the British North America Act"	75
The British North America Act does not break "the continuity of the prescriptive rights and traditions of the respective Provinces" . .	76
The difference between Legislatures and Municipal Corporations . .	77
The powers and immunities of the Legislative Assembly of Lower Canada, and of the late Province of Canada, attach to the Legislative Assembly of Quebec.	79
The Legislative Assembly of Quebec "has not the mere nude power of Legislation"	80
Remarks of Baron Parke in Kielly *vs.* Carson, respecting the right of a Legislative Assembly to protect itself.	80

CHAPTER XIV.

The continuity of the Provincial powers	82
Mr. Justice Monk's remarks on the subject	82-85

CHAPTER XV.

Limitation of the powers of the Federal and Local Parliaments . . .	85
Difference between the powers of the Imperial and Federal Parliaments	85

Index.   ix.

	PAGE
The Oaths Bill of the Federal Parliament; the Queen's disallowance thereof	86
The Legislatures of Quebec and Ontario pass Oaths Bills which become law	86
"The privileges," etc., of the Senate and House of Commons defined	87
The claim of the Speaker of the Imperial House of Commons to rights and privileges	87–88
The claim of the Speaker of the Ontario Parliament to the same	88
The powers of the Federal Parliament; they are not sovereign	89
The powers of the Imperial Parliament	89–90

CHAPTER XVI.

The "omnipotence" of the Federal Parliament dispelled	91
Hon. Edward Blake's opinion on the "omnipotence" of the Federal Parliament	91
The Courts could enquire into the question whether the Federal Parliament had exceeded its powers	92
How the Provinces can baffle Federal usurpation	92
They can apply for an amendment of the Constitution	93

CHAPTER XVII.

Prerogative claims set aside; Constitutional victory for Ontario and Quebec	93
Report of Col. Bernard, Deputy Minister of Justice, against the Ontario Act, "to amend the Law of Escheats," etc.	93–96
Hon. Attorney-General Mowat's reply	97
He maintains that Provincial rights, not given to the Dominion by the British North America Act, are retained by the Provinces	98
His definition of Escheat	100
His exposition of prerogative rights	101–104
Hon. Mr. Fournier, Minister of Justice, replies to Attorney-General Mowat	104–106
Disallowance of the Act	106
The question again opened; Hon. Edward Blake's memorandum on the subject	106–108
He makes certain recommendations	108–109
Decision of the five Judges, Queen's Bench, Quebec, in favour of that Province, in a question of Escheat	109–111
Hon. Attorney-General Mowat's answer to the memorandum of the Minister of Justice	112

CHAPTER XVIII.

	PAGE
The Provincial appointment of Queen's Counsel	112
Sir John A. Macdonald's report on the subject	113
The questions he propounds for the Law Officers of the Crown	115
The answers of the Law Officers	115–116
Offer of the Dominion Government to the Queen's Counsel for Ontario, proposing to grant them Federal Commissions	117–118
Minute of Council of the Ontario Government on the action of the Federal Government *in re* the opinion of the Law Officers	118
Opinion of the Ontario Government that these appointments pertain to the Local and not to the Federal Government	119
Reply of the Federal Government to the Minute of the Ontario Government	119–121
Ontario Act respecting the appointment of Queen's Counsel	121
Preamble to this Act	121
The authority for the passing of this Act, and for the Act to regulate the precedence of the Bar of Ontario	121

CHAPTER XIX.

Who are the present Queen's Counsel in Ontario?	123
The supporters of the Provincial right to appoint Queen's Counsel—Sir John A. Macdonald, the Law Officers, Hon. Edward Blake, Hon. O. Mowat	123

CHAPTER XX.

Can the Governor-General appoint Queen's Counsel?	125
No authority to make these appointments conferred on Lord Sydenham, Sir E. Head or Lord Monck	125
Extract from the Commission to Marquis of Lorne	126
Judicial opinion that Queen's Counsel are not officers of the Courts	127
Consolidated Statutes of Upper Canada on this point	127
The Federal Parliament can confer on the Governor-General the power to appoint Queen's Counsel	128
Limitation of the prerogative in the Colonies	128–131
Status of a Queen's Counsel appointed by the Governor-General	131
The title unrecognized in "Rules of Precedence"	131–132

CHAPTER XXI.

Are the Provinces Republics?	133
Citations from the British North America Act on the subject	133–134

	PAGE
Mr. Alpheus Todd's opinion	134–135
Extract from Earl of Dufferin's Commission	135
Earl of Beaconsfield's opinion	136
The Crown has abandoned practical prerogative in Canada	137
Imperial Parliament abolishes power of English Courts to issue writs of *Habeas Corpus* into Canada	137

CHAPTER XXII.

The Queen's name in Provincial Legislation	138
Its omission would not invalidate Provincial Acts	138
Precedents in the case of the Thirteen Colonies	138
Enacting part of an Act in the Assembly of Virginia, when belonging to the Empire	138
Enacting part of an Act of the Assembly of Massachusetts Bay	138–139
Enacting part of an Act in the Province of New York and in the Province of Georgia	139
Enacting part of an Act in the Dominion, the Province of Ontario and Province of Quebec	140–141
"An Act of Assembly has the same effect in the Colonies as an Act of Parliament has in the Mother Country"	140–141

CHAPTER XXIII.

The struggle and triumph of the Legislature of Jamaica	141
The Legislature of Jamaica appoint a Committee to inquire into a mutiny	142
The Duke of Manchester, the Governor of the Island, is requested to lay before the Committee the proceedings of the Courts-Martial	142
The Duke lays before the House the letter of Major-General Carmichael, Commander of the Forces, declining to deliver the proceedings of the Courts-Martial	143
The Committee request the Governor to ask for the attendance of two officers of the regiment which had mutinied	143
The officers attend the Committee, but a general order issued by Major-General Carmichael forbids their giving evidence	143–144
Whereupon the House passes six Resolutions	144–145–146
The Speaker issues his warrant for the attendance of Major-General Carmichael at the Bar	146
He declines to attend at the Bar	146–147
The House orders him to be arrested for contempt	147–148
The House passes three Resolutions which are sent to the Governor,	148–149

	PAGE
The Governor thereupon prorogues the House, in order to consult the Imperial authorities	149
The House re-assembles	150
The Governor informs the House that the King has ordered the proceedings of the Courts-Martial to be laid before them	150
Arrest of Major-General Carmichael	151
He appears at the Bar of the House; explains and is discharged	151
Address of the House to the Governor	152
"Every right and privilege exercised by the Commons House of Parliament" are claimed by the Jamaica Legislature	152

CHAPTER XXIV.

The Magna Charta of the British Colonies	153
Lord Abingdon's opinion on the Declaratory Act	153-154
Citations from the Declaratory Act	154
The King and Parliament of Great Britain "will not impose any duty, tax, or assessment in any of the Colonies"	154-155

CHAPTER XXV.

The dangers of Federal centralization	155

APPENDIX No. 1.

Definition of "Legislature"	157

APPENDIX No. 2.

Expenditure for Civil Government in Ontario and Canada	157-158

APPENDIX No. 3.

A Colonial Secretary pronounces against a Court of Appeal	158-159

APPENDIX No. 4.

The Local Legislature	159-160

THE POWERS OF
CANADIAN PARLIAMENTS.

CHAPTER I.

PARLIAMENTS AND LEGISLATURES.

THE purpose of this volume is to show that the present Legislatures of Ontario and Quebec are the political heirs-at-law of the old historical Parliaments of Upper and Lower Canada, and of the late Province of United Canada. Its object is also to make manifest that these Legislatures of Ontario and Quebec inherit the powers of the Representative Bodies which preceded them; and that they were established, and that they exist to perform the functions and duties which render necessary the life of a Colonial Parliament.

It may be necessary to inquire by what titles our Canadian Legislatures have, in times past, designated themselves; how they understood their functions; how they claimed and vindicated their privileges.

Lieutenant-Governor Gore, in a proclamation respecting the Prorogation of Parliament, dated York, April 10th, 1811, issues an address:

"To our beloved and faithful Legislative Councillors of

our Province of Upper Canada, and to our Knights, Citizens, and Burgesses of our said Province, to the Provincial Parliament, at our town of York."

In an official document, issued by Sir Peregrine Maitland, dated York, 21st of October, 1826, are found the words :—" Whereas, by our proclamation, bearing date the 25th day of September last, we thought fit to prorogue our Provincial Parliament," etc.

The Legislature of the late Province of Canada was, throughout its history, styled, in official documents, " The Provincial Parliament." In the Journals of the old House of Assembly, of 1854, we find a proclamation of the Earl of Elgin dissolving " the present Provincial Parliament of Our said Province."

In the Confederation Resolutions, seventy-two in number, adopted on the 13th of March, 1865, by the late Parliament of Canada, we find that the words "Legislature," and " Parliament," " House of Commons," and " House of Assembly," are regarded as practically synonymous and interchangeable.

Resolution 6. " There shall be a General Legislature or Parliament for the Federated Provinces, composed of the Legislative Council and the House of Commons."

Resolution 49. " The House of Commons, or House of Assembly shall not originate," etc.

Resolution 79. "The sanction of Imperial and Local Parliaments shall be sought for the Union of the Provinces," etc.

In the earlier years of Confederation, the proclamations

respecting the summoning of the Houses of Ontario and Quebec, employed the words " Legislature or Parliament of the Province of Ontario ;" and " Legislature or Parliament of the Province of Quebec."

A despatch, 29th March, 1877, from the Earl of Carnarvon, Secretary of State for the Colonies, was sent to the Earl of Dufferin, concerning the validity of Acts done under the Great Seal of Nova Scotia. In this communication the Earl of Carnarvon makes use of the following words :—

" I am advised . . . that the Local Legislature, with the previous assent of the Crown, is competent to empower the Lieut.-Governor to alter the Seal, meaning by the term ' Local Legislature,' the Legislature of the Dominion."

It is true that, by the 69th section of the British North America Act, it is provided that " There shall be a Legislature for Ontario, consisting of the Lieutenant-Governor and of one House, styled the Legislative Assembly of Ontario." But the authorities already cited, in illustration of the use of the words, " Parliament" and " Legislature," furnish abundant justification of the employment throughout this book, of these twin terms as absolute equivalents.

After all, however, this is not so much a question of words, as it is of the interpretation to be placed on the functions of the Federal and Provincial Legislatures ; and upon the extent and limitation of their respective powers. For, in the technical precision of constitutional terminology, it is a question whether the word Parliament, in all the far-reaching significance of the term, comprehending, as it does, powers and attributes which, for purposes of Government, are practically uncircumscribed, should not be restricted alone to the Imperial Legislature of Great Britain and Ireland.

CHAPTER II.

THE PRIVILEGES OF THE PARLIAMENT OF UPPER CANADA.

ON the 17th of September, 1792, the first Parliament of Upper Canada met at Newark, now known as Niagara. Lieutenant-Governor Simcoe delivered to them an address, the opening paragraph of which said :—

"I have summoned you together under the authority of an Act of the Parliament of Great Britain, passed in the last year, and which has established the British Constitution, and also the forms which secure and maintain it in this distant country."

Mr John McDonnell, the member for Glengarry, was elected Speaker. Following the English custom, he presented himself for approval to Lieutenant-Governor Simcoe. Thereupon the King's Representative promised that the members of the House should "enjoy freedom of debate, access to his person, and freedom from arrest."

Doubts have been raised as to the validity of Simcoe's words. But the difficulty is, after all, a mere question of phrases. The great self-evident fact remains unassailed and unassailable, that the Legislature of the Province of Upper Canada, as long as it existed, continued to do things pertaining to a Parliament. It raised money by taxes; made, enforced and repealed laws; exercised the right to arrest and imprison. In a word, the Upper Canadian Legislature, in its local sphere, was as much a Parliament as, in its imperial sphere, was the House of Commons in Westminster.

We shall see, in another place, whether, in the opinion of some of our ablest jurists, the rights and powers of the old Parliaments have not descended to the present legislatures of Ontario and Quebec. In the meantime we shall glance at some of the acts of the Parliament of Upper Canada; acts in which it exercised powers that were locally sovereign; which powers were never abrogated or questioned by the King's representative, or denied by the King's Courts.

The Statute of 31st George the Third, cap. 31, known as the "Constitutional Act," authorized the division of the Province of Quebec into the separate Provinces of Upper and Lower Canada; and the establishment of their respective Legislatures. The second section of this Act provides amongst other things, "That in each of the said Provinces His Majesty, His Heirs and Successors, shall have power during the continuance of this Act, by and with the advice and consent of the Legislative Assembly of such

Provinces, respectively, *to make laws for the peace, welfare, and good government thereof,"* etc.

The words "peace, welfare and good government" occur first in an Order in Council, dated "At the Court at Kensington, the 31st of December, 1696." The Order, before declaring the approbation of the King, in Council, of certain laws passed in "the General Assembly of His Majesty's Island of Montserrat," proceeds :—

"Whereas His Majesty has been pleased by His Royal Commission, of October 26, 1689, to authorize the Governor, Councils, and Assemblies of their Majesty's Leeward Charibee Islands in America, jointly and severally to make, constitute and ordain laws, statutes and ordinances, for the public peace, welfare and good government of the said Islands," etc.

We shall now proceed to show how the Parliament of Upper Canada interpreted the privileges which it maintained had been conceded by Lieut.-Governor Simcoe, on the founding a new National Legislature in the wilderness.

PRIVILEGE PLEADED AGAINST ARREST.

The following are illustrations from the Journals of the Legislative Assembly and Council for 1812.

Mr. Alex. McDonnell, member for Glengarry, on the 11th of February, 1812, complained, by letter to the House, that Mr. William W. Baldwin had grossly violated its privileges. The offence of Mr. Baldwin was that, as

---

* Stokes, on the Constitution of the British Colonies in North America and the West Indies. London, 1783.

Deputy Clerk of the Crown, he had, in July, 1811, as an Attorney, issued a writ of *capias* to the Sheriff of the Home District for the arrest of Mr. McDonnell. It was also charged against Mr. Baldwin that he had, when warned by the Deputy Sheriff that Mr. McDonnell, as a member of the House, was privileged from arrest, denied that claim, and insisted on the arrest. But the Deputy Sheriff refused to act, and so with the Sheriff. It so happened that Mr. Baldwin was an officer of the Legislative Council; this fact, in the opinion of Mr. McDonnell, added to the offence of breach of privilege of the House of Assembly, a branch of the same Legislature.

Mr. Baldwin was pronounced guilty of a breach of privilege. The Legislative Council, having been informed of the action of the Assembly, peremptorily dismissed him from his office as Master in Chancery. But the Assembly was easily pacified; and, at its instance, the Legislative Council reinstated Mr. Baldwin.

THE CASE OF MR. NICHOL AND CHIEF JUSTICE SCOTT.

On the 20th of February, 1812, the House

Resolved, That Robert Nichol has been guilty of a breach of the privileges of this House; by making a false, malicious and scandalous representation to the person administering the Government,* relative to the proceedings of this House, contained in his letter of the 25th of April, 1811, accompanying his road accounts, and

---

* Major-General Brock.

also by words used in the presence of a member of this House.

The House then authorized Mr. Samuel Street, the Speaker, to issue his warrant, to the Sergeant-at-Arms, for the arrest of Mr. Robert Nichol, of the Township of Woodhouse, "to answer unto such matters and things as may then and there be objected against him, touching a contempt of the privileges of this House, with which he stands charged, and abide by the pleasure of the House thereon."

On the 26th of February, Mr. Robert Nichol was brought to the Bar of the House.

Mr. Sovereign, a member, "gave evidence of words used by Mr. Nichol, in his presence, disrespectful to the House of Assembly." Mr. Willcocks, another member, gave evidence similar to that of Mr. Sovereign.

Mr. Nichol was then heard in his defence; whereupon it was

Resolved, That Mr. Nichol has been guilty of a breach of privilege, in addition to his former offence, by denying that this House have the privilege of committing an offender, who by them has been found guilty of a breach of privilege.

It was resolved that Mr. Nichol be committed to the common gaol of the district, during the pleasure of the House, and that the Speaker do issue his warrant for that purpose.

The Speaker then read the warrant, which he signed by order of the House. It was as follows:—

"Samuel Street, Esquire, Speaker of the Honourable Commons House of Assembly,

"To the Sheriff of the Home District: Greeting :—

"By virtue of the power and authority in me vested by the Honourable Commons House of Assembly, you are hereby ordered and required to receive into the common gaol of your district, the body of Robert Nichol, and him safely keep during the pleasure of this House, the said Robert Nichol having been convicted of a breach of privilege of the Commons House of Assembly.

"Given under my hand and seal, at York, this 26th day of February, 1812.

"SAMUEL STREET,
"*Speaker.*

" "COMMONS HOUSE OF ASSEMBLY."

On the 29th of February, 1812, Mr. John Beikie, Sheriff of the Home District, stated to the House that he had received into the gaol the body of Robert Nichol by virtue of the warrant of the Speaker; but that the prisoner has since been brought up by writ of *Habeas Corpus*, before Chief Justice Scott, and was by him liberated.

The House thereupon resolved :—

"That the Honourable Thomas Scott, Chief Justice of this Province, has been guilty of a violent breach of the privileges of this House, by discharging from the gaol of this district, the body of Robert Nichol who was committed to prison for having committed a breach of the privileges of the House."

The House then sent a message to the Legislative Council, informing them of the course they had taken respecting Chief Justice Scott, and requesting them to proceed in the matter as the nature of the case required. The Chief Justice was Speaker of the Legislative Council.

On the 2nd of March, 1812, in the Legislative Council Chamber:

"The Resolutions of the Commons House of Assembly on the 20th of February, 1812, brought up this day to this House by Message, having been read.

"It is considered that this House disclaim any right to interfere with the proceedings of the Chief Justice, in the exercise of his judicial functions; but he, as Speaker of this House, having thought proper to enter into an explanation of his conduct in the matter stated in the aforesaid resolution, it is ordered that his explanation, so given, shall be entered upon the Journals of this House, and a copy thereof sent to the Commons House of Assembly.

"The Chief Justice is bound, by his office, to grant *Habeas Corpus*, and to discharge the prisoner, if the commitment appears, on the return, to be illegal.

"To enable the Judges to decide on the legality of a commitment, it was the law of the land that every warrant of commitment should contain upon the face of it the cause.

"The High Court or the King in Council, having neglected in some orders of commitment to insert the special cause, and the Judges scrupling to relieve by *Habeas Corpus*, at Common Law, on account of the high dignity of the Court in which the King himself sat in person, a Statute was passed in the 16th Chas. I. whereby by it is enacted that the Judges shall grant *Habeas Corpus* on all commitments by His Majesty in Council; and if, upon the return, it does not appear to be for just and legal cause, they shall, under heavy penalties, bail or discharge.

"Since the Statute, it has become part of the law and usage of Parliament that all warrants of commitment, by the House of Commons, do specify the cause and recite the particular privilege, or breach whereof the party has, by the House, been adjudged guilty: and also the specific order of the House for his imprisonment. Without such adjudication and order by the House, the Speaker has no authority; and his authority must be shown in order to render his warrant valid.

"It appears by warrants of the Speakers of the House of Commons in England, at two different periods within an interval of forty years, that the usage of the House of Commons is conformable to the exigence of the Statute, with respect to the High Court of the King in Council.

"These warrants show, distinctly, the particular privilege violated, the judgment of the House upon the charge, the time when that adjudication was made, the Order of the House for the specific punishment, and the date of that Order, whereupon, and not otherwise, the

Speaker can require the detention of the offender, in custody of any gaoler.

"This reasonable proceeding shows a charge, a trial and adjudication, a sentence and award of execution, from all which the Court or Judge can decide if it is legal or not. From a copy of the return on the writ of *Habeas Corpus* sued out by Mr. Nichol, it does not appear of what nature was the breach of privilege charged; how, when, or where he had been adjudged guilty, or that his imprisonment was ordered by the House.

"The warrant under which Mr. Nichol was detained appeared in all respects as the personal act of Mr. Street, under his seal, supposing authority vested in him personally by the House of Assembly.

"Such an authority cannot be delegated. Whatever powers the House of Assembly may have to decide upon their own privileges, it must be exercised by the House itself, as a House, and not by the Speaker in his own person. And, as the Chief Justice had only the return of the *Habeas Corpus* before him, wherein the said warrant was inserted, and the warrant being materially defective, he was bound to discharge the prisoner. No question, therefore, respecting privilege could arise.

"(Signed)   JOHN POWELL,
"*Clerk Legislative Council.*"

On the 4th of March, 1812, in the House of Assembly, the following motion was adopted :—

" That, as the Legislative Council, by their Message of the 2nd of March, disclaimed any right to interfere with the conduct of the Hon. Chief Justice Scott, guilty of a breach of the privileges of this House, which they allege not to be done as a member of their House, but in his character as a Judge—notwithstanding that they did interfere during this present session and punish an officer of their House upon complaint of this—it therefore becomes the duty of this House to vindicate its rights and privileges in the manner which shall appear to it best calculated to preserve them."

Then an address to the Prince Regent was adopted. It is in part as follows :—

" An imperious sense of duty urges us to state to your Royal Highness, that an alarming, dangerous and unjustifiable violation of the privileges of the Commons of this Province has lately been made by the Hon. Thomas Scott, His Majesty's Chief Justice, inasmuch as he liberated from prison Mr. Robert Nichol, who had been committed by them for a high contempt and breach of their privileges. Such an interference, on the part of the judicial authority, we cannot too much deprecate, impressed as we are with the important consequences resulting from it in the Representative Body of the people of this Colony.

"We therefore humbly pray that your Royal Highness will be graciously pleased to propose such measures as in your wisdom may be deemed the most proper and efficient to afford us prompt redress.

"(Signed)   SAMUEL STREET,
"*Speaker.*

"COMMONS HOUSE OF ASSEMBLY,
"*4th of March, 1812.*"

On the 6th of March, 1812, the day of the prorogation, Major-General Brock, the President Administering the Government of Upper Canada, assured the House of Assembly that he should not fail to transmit to His Majesty's principal Secretary of State, those addresses intended to be laid before the Prince Regent.*

It will be seen from the foregoing proceedings, that Chief Justice Scott did not contest the power of the House to vindicate its privileges. The exception which he took was as to the objectionable form of the Speaker's warrant of commitment. "The warrant being materially defective, he was bound to discharge the prisoner. No question, therefore, respecting privilege could arise."

---

* Journals of the House of Assembly and Legislative Council, 1812.

CHAPTER III.

THE CASE OF MESSRS. COFFIN AND GIVENS.

WE shall again proceed to show, in the language of official documents themselves, how the Legislatures of Upper Canada interpreted the words we have italicised, viz., " *To make laws for the peace, welfare and good government of the Province of Canada.*" In the Journals of the House of Assembly of Upper Canada, 1828, are found :

Motion, that Nathaniel Coffin, Esq., Adjutant-General of Militia, and James Givens, Esq., Superintendent of Indian Affairs, having been summoned by a Committee to appear before them, and not having complied therewith, they be apprehended and placed at the Bar, to answer for such contempt, forthwith. Amendment, for appointing a Committee to search into precedents, and ascertain in what cases the Executive Government should be addressed, in order to produce the attendance of any public officer, etc., negatived : main motion agreed to. Sergeant-at-Arms reports his proceedings upon the Speaker's warrant, and the refusal of those gentlemen to allow themselves to be arrested ; Report ordered to be entered upon the Journals, *nem. con.* They are placed at the Bar, and, being called upon for their defence, they severally explain the cause of their refusal; their statements to be taken down in writing, and entered on the Journals. Motion, that James Givens, Esq., has been guilty of contempt of the House, and a breach of its privileges, and that the Speaker do issue his warrant for committing him to the York Gaol for the remainder of the present Session: several amendments negatived, and motion agreed to. A like resolution, respecting Nathaniel Coffin, Esq. Speaker submits the form of separate warrants of committal, which are approved by the House. Sergeant-at-Arms directed to carry the same into execution.

The plea of Messrs. Coffin and Givens was, that both of them had applied to Sir P. Maitland for leave to attend the Committee, but that, in each case, he had refused permission. In the case of Mr. Givens, his Excellency's answer was, "That he is an officer of the Indian Department, and is now acting as the head of that Department in this Province." In the case of Mr. Coffin, his answer was, that he could not give him permission to attend the Committee, appointed to inquire and report upon the petition of William Forsyth, because he (the Lieut.-Governor) did not know what were the matters of which Forsyth complained, or what were the facts in regard to which the Committee desired to interrogate Mr. Coffin.

In respect of these arrests, a Message was transmitted to the House of Assembly, by the Lieutenant-Governor, Sir Peregrine Maitland. Mr. Speaker Willson, who, in his signature to the Address in reply to the Speech from the Throne, at the opening of the Session, styles himself " John Willson, Speaker, *Commons* House of Assembly," read the Message to the House :

" P. MAITLAND. The Lieutenant-Governor acquaints the House of Assembly that the Adjutant-General of Militia, and Colonel Givens, Superintendent of Indian Affairs, acting as the head of that Department in this Province, have reported to him that they are in custody under a warrant of the Speaker of the House of Assembly for a contempt in disobeying the summons of a Select Committee appointed to report upon a petition of William Forsyth.

"The Lieutenant-Governor will always view with extreme regret any circumstance likely to produce misunderstanding between any of the branches of the Legislature ; and, notwithstanding the protection which he justly owes to all officers serving under his Government, and acting, as he conceives, in the due discharge of their duty, he has forborne to interrupt the proceedings of the Session, by hastening the intended period of Prorogation,* indulging a hope that some measure useful to the country might be matured before the Legislature separated.

. . . .

" The departure of the Assembly from the usage prevailing in this Colony, and as far as he can learn, in

---

* This expression is somewhat obscure : it may mean, however, that, although the prorogation of the House would, of necessity, have liberated the officials, the Lieut.-Governor had forborne to hasten that event.

other Governments, could not be acquiesced in by him without that conviction of its propriety which he does not now entertain.*

"For his future guidance, under similar circumstances, he will solicit the directions of His Majesty's Government—if the power claimed by the House of Assembly has been constitutionally assumed and exercised, the House has discharged its duty in asserting it. If, otherwise, the Lieutenant-Governor, in withholding his permission,† had a duty to fulfil from which he could not properly recede—and of this the Assembly may be assured, that if the propriety of its proceedings shall be confirmed by His Majesty, no one will be more ready than himself to recognize the privilege in question on all future occasions, and to enforce its observance by all whom it is his duty to control.

"GOVERNMENT HOUSE,
  "*24th March, 1828.*"

This Message from Sir Peregrine Maitland is nothing less than might be expected from one who cherished his peculiar views on what we now term Responsible Government. The second paragraph ends with a sneer. It is to be observed, however, that the complaint is a personal one; the House had dared to imprison two officers whom the Lieutenant-Governor regarded as under his

---

* Sir P. G. Maitland was unaware of the case of the Legislature of Jamaica and Major-General Carmichael, noticed in another place.

† To obey the summons of the Committee.

protection, " acting as they conceived, in the due discharge of their duty."

But the most important point yet remains to be noticed. There can be no doubt that Sir Peregrine fulfilled his promise " to solicit the direction of His Majesty's Government." There can be as little doubt, that no official answer to the "solicitation" was ever made public. The Imperial Government, by its silence, must be taken to have acquiesed in the course of the Upper Canadian Legislature. The House took no action on the Message. Messrs. Givens and Coffin were committed on the 22nd of March; the House was prorogued on the 25th of March, when, of course, they would be liberated.

THE CASE OF MR. ALLAN MACNAB.

In the House, in 1829: *

"Motion, that Allan N. MacNab, Esq., having refused to answer certain questions put to him by the Committee on the Hamilton Outrage, and having otherwise misdemeaned himself, is guilty of a high contempt and breach of the Privileges of the House. Motion agreed to. Mr. Speaker to issue his warrant for apprehending him. He is placed at the Bar, and called on for his defence, which he makes accordingly. Motion, that Mr. MacNab be discharged; amendment, that he be committed to York Gaol, during the pleasure of the House, carried. The Speaker submits a warrant of committal which is approved by the House. Mr. Speaker reports a letter from Mr. MacNab, relative to his imprisonment. Order, that he be

* Journals, 1829.

discharged. Mr. Speaker submits a warrant for his discharge, which was approved of."

We have seen how the Legislatures of Upper Canada defined and maintained their privileges. Let us now see in what light the Jurists regarded these claims. We shall take the case of *MacNab* v. *Bidwell and Baldwin*, as reported in Draper's King Bench Reports, Easter Term, 1830; pp. 144-158.

The Court held that "the House of Assembly in this Province have a constitutional right to call persons before them for the purpose of obtaining information; and if the House adjudge the conduct of such persons in answering or refusing to answer before a Select Committee to be a contempt, they have the right of imprisoning them." The charge was trespass and false imprisonment against the Speaker, and another member of the House of Assembly, Mr. Baldwin. Chief Justice the Hon. John Beverley Robinson, in delivering judgment, said amongst other things :—

. . . "In a case, then, of contempt, so clearly and directly alleged on the pleadings, and resolved by the House, I cannot see upon what sound principle the power of the Assembly can be denied. . . . Then, if *a priori*, and independently of precedents, such a body as the House of Commons must be armed with authority to commit for contempt, and thereby to remove any immediate obstructions to its proceedings, I think the same power, for the same reasons, must be admitted to reside in the House of

Assembly here: for that Assembly represents all the people in this Province; it has, in conjunction with the other branches of the Legislature, *power to bind the lives, liberties and estates of all the inhabitants of this country:**

"Although the Legislature of this Colony is subordinate to the Imperial Parliament, it is the *supreme power* acting in this Province; *its legislative authority extends to the most important objects*, and the instances in which it is restrained, are, perhaps, not those of the greatest and most immediate consequence for the welfare of society. If a legislative body with such powers, and established for such purposes, had not also the power of giving effect to their consultations, by protecting themselves from insult, and removing obstruction from their proceedings, I am not certain that more injury than good might not be found to result from the Constitution conferred upon us; and I cannot satisfy myself, upon any reasoning, that it is not as important for us as the people of England that our Legislature should not be compelled to make laws in the dark, and that they should have power to inquire before they come to decide. : . . .

"Without discussing further the objections that have been or may be raised, I am, on the whole, of opinion that this action cannot be supported. . . . . It is plain that if upon this record this action could be sustained against one of those defendants, no one could venture hereafter to fill the situation of Speaker; and if it could be sustained against the other, certainly that would be an end

---

* The italics here, and elsewhere in this decision, are our own.

of an independent exercise of the will and judgment upon constitutional questions by the members of that body.

. . . .

"The true point of view in which to regard the question is, that these powers are required by the House in order to enable them to promote the welfare of their constituents; we are bound to suppose that they will use them with discretion and for good ends, and, *if we had the power*, we should have no right to withhold them, on the assumption that they desire to pervert the objects of their Constitution."

Judgment for defendants.

CASE OF SOLICITOR-GENERAL BOULTON.

"Mr. Henry John Boulton, Solicitor-General: For a high contempt and breach of the Privileges of the House, in objecting to answer questions put to him by the Committee on the Hamilton Outrage. He is placed at the Bar, and makes his defence. He is admonished and discharged. Order, *nem. con.*, for placing on the Journals what Mr. Speaker (Bidwell) said in admonishing him."

The Speaker, in his admonition to the Solicitor-General, amongst other things, said:—

"The privileges of the House of Assembly, which you have questioned, have been given to it by the Constitution, and for wise and useful purposes. They are necessary for the preservation of its rights and the performance of its most important duties. It is the Grand Inquest of the Province. It is not merely allowed, but bound, to inquire into all grievances and abuses, and to remedy them; especially those which, from the rank, influence, or number of delinquents, or from any other circumstances, the ordinary tribunals of justice cannot fully and promptly redress. These privileges, therefore, are necessary for the protection of the people and the welfare of the country.

"It is to the spirit and firmness with which the House of Commons in England has upon all occasions asserted and maintained its Privileges against the King and the House of Lords, and, when necessary, against popular prejudice, that our parent country owes her liberties and the best principles of her Constitution. They must be as necessary for the protection of the subject, and the preservation of liberty in this Province, as they ever have been in England. They should be guarded and supported, therefore, with the same vigilance and resolution here as they have been in that country—whose example it is our pride and duty to follow.

. . . .

" Finding, from your answer, that you are now disposed to treat its Privileges with just and becoming respect, and to defer your own private opinion to the judgment of that body whose Constitutional right it is to decide upon its own Privileges, it is willing to dismiss you with no other punishment than this admonition from its Speaker. This moderation is a proof that these Privileges have been safely lodged by the Constitution in its hands, and that they will never be used in a wanton or oppressive manner."*

---

* Journals, 1829.

CHAPTER IV.

THE PARLIAMENT OF UPPER CANADA IN ADVANCE OF THE IMPERIAL PARLIAMENT: THE PUBLIC ACCOUNTS.

Mr. Alpheus Todd, in his invaluable work on "Parliamentary Government in England,"* in narrating the history of the formation of the Committee on Public Accounts, speaks of its creation thus :—

"And this brings us to the mention of the crowning act, whereby the House of Commons has been enabled to exercise a constitutional control over the public expenditure, without infringing upon the functions of responsible ministers ; that is to say through the instrumentality of a Standing Committee of its own members."

This "crowning act" was performed by the Parliament of Upper Canada, exactly half a century before the Imperial Parliament carried it into operation.

On the 7th of February, 1812, in the Legislative Assembly of Upper Canada, a Select Committee was appointed to "Inspect the Public Accounts, and report the same to this House."

The Report of the Committee, which bears evidence of being carefully prepared, was submitted to the House on the 2nd of March, 1812.

On March 31st, 1862, the House of Commons appointed "A Standing Committee, styled 'The Committee of Public

---
* Vol. 1, pp. 588-593.

Accounts,' for the examination of the Accounts, showing the appropriation of the sums granted by Parliament to meet the Public Expenditure."*

CHAPTER V.

PRIVILEGE IN THE PROVINCE OF LOWER CANADA.

WE shall now inquire how the Legislature of the Province of Lower Canada understood and vindicated its privileges. The plea of privilege as against arrest was tested in the second Session of the new Legislature, called into existence by the Constitutional Act of 1791.

On the 27th of November, 1793, Speaker Panet read to the House of Assembly of Lower Canada,† a letter he had received from Mr John Young, a member thereof.

The letter bore date, " Quebec, Monday morning, Nov. 25th, 1793." It reminded the Speaker that, at the opening of the present Legislature, he, in the name of the House of Assembly, ' claimed such privileges and liberties as are enjoyed by the Commons of Great Britain ; and His Majesty, by his Representatives, having recognized the enjoyment of all just rights and lawful privileges, I think it necessary to inform you that, on Saturday afternoon, the Sheriff of Quebec, by one of his officers, arrested my person, upon a writ of *Capias ad respondendum*, issued out of the Court of Common Pleas, on the 23rd inst., by

---
* Todd, Vol. 1, pp. 588-593. † Journals of the House, 1793-94.

James Hunt, of Quebec, Ironmonger, upon a declaration signed by J. A. Panet.

"As a private individual and a merchant, . . . I submitted to the arrest, and gave bail; but, in my public character, as a member of the House of Assembly, it is also my duty to inform the House of this contempt and infraction of their privileges.

"I have, therefore, to request of you to lay this information before the House, in whose hands, according to the Constitution, is lodged the vindication of their own rights; that the House may have a knowledge of the insult offered to them through me, and be enabled to take such measures as they shall see expedient to punish such a violation of their constitutional privileges.

"JOHN YOUNG."

On the 7th of January, 1794, the House

Resolved, That the person of John Young, Esquire, a Member of Assembly, was arrested on the 23rd of November last, in direct violation of the undoubted rights and privileges of this House.

On the 8th of January, 1794, the House, in a series of Resolutions, found guilty of a breach of privilege, James Hunt, who instituted the suit against Mr. Young; J. A. Panet, the Speaker of the House, who acted as Advocate for Hunt; Sheriff Shepherd, who authorized the bailiff to serve the writ, and the bailiff for making the arrest.

On the 9th of January, 1794, the Speaker put the following question to the House :—

"Whether it be the pleasure of this Honourable House

that he be permitted to declare, and cause to be inserted in the Journals, his apology and submission to the Resolution of this House, concerning the arrest of John Young, Esquire." Passed unanimously.

The Speaker then read the following declaration in both languages :—

"As the Honourable House have judged necessary to resolve, that I am guilty of a breach of its privileges, in regard to the arrest of John Young, Esq., one of its Members, I consider it to be my duty to submit, personally, to the resolution of the majority of this House ; and at the same time, to express with candour, . . . that I had not any intention in the charge I undertook, as Advocate for James Hunt, in the action which he instituted against John Young, Esq., to infringe or violate the privileges of this House; but that I conceived, in the month of November last, that the laws of this country authorized the arrest. . . . I hope this Honourable House will accept this apology and excuse me, if in the commencement of such a Constitution as ours, my opinions in law, as an Advocate, have not had the good fortune to meet those of the majority of this Honourable House. The error was involuntary ; it is established by the Resolution of this House ; I submit to its Resolve ; and, as a further proof of which I declare, that this morning, I fyled, in the Court of Common Pleas, of Quebec, a petition, of which I now produce a copy, to have leave to desist from prosecuting, as Advocate, the cause in court, until that the arrest of John Young, Esq., or his special bail be discharged.

"J. A. PANET."

Resolved, That the apology and declaration just made by the Speaker, are sufficient and satisfactory to this House, and that, in consequence, no further proceedings be taken on the Resolution which concerns him.

On the 10th of January, 1794, the House ordered that James Hunt be taken into the custody of the Serjeant-at-Arms, there to remain till he has caused the bail given by Mr. James Young, a member of this Assembly, to be discharged; and further, till he has made satisfaction to this House for the breach of the privileges thereof; and that Mr. Speaker do issue his warrant accordingly.

On the 13th of January, Sheriff Shepherd presented himself at the Bar of the House, and made his apology. It was then resolved that, as he had made satisfaction to the House for the breach of the privileges thereof, by him committed, no other proceedings be had on the Resolution regarding him.

On the 14th of January, the bailiff, one Hooper, made his apology at the Bar of the House, whereupon the same order was made in his case as in that of the Sheriff, his superior.

PRIVILEGE PLEADED AGAINST JURY SERVICE.

On the 19th of February, 1795, five members, Messrs. Lees, Lester, Young, Grant and Duniere, complained to the House that, in breach of its privileges, Sheriff Shepherd did, on the 18th inst., cause them, members of this House, to be served with summonses to appear as Special Jurors at the Court of King's Bench.

The House resolved that the members aforesaid "have privilege not to serve" as Special Jurors "and that a letter be written by Mr. Speaker to the Judges, that they may not be amerced for their non-appearance."

On the 21st of February, the Speaker, Mr. C. De Lotbinière, informed the house that he had written to the Judges of the Court of King's Bench, in the sense of the foregoing Resolution.*

The Judges recognized that the members "have privilege not to serve," for there was no further trouble in the matter.

EXPULSION OF A MEMBER.

On the 31st of March, 1800, the order for taking into consideration the copy of the Record of the proceedings upon the indictment, in the Court of King's Bench, Montreal, against Charles Baptiste Bouc, Esq., a member of this House; and also for the said M. Bouc's attending in his place, being read, the House proceeded to take the same into consideration.

The copy of the Record of the proceedings in the King's Bench was read.

M. Bouc, attending in his place, pursuant to the order of the House, was heard in his defence, and afterwards withdrew.

On the 2nd of April, 1800, it was

Resolved, That this House, by their Resolution of Monday last, having voted that it appeared to this House by a Record of the Court of King's Bench, Mon-

---

* Journals, 1795.

treal, then read, that Charles Baptiste Bouc, a member of this House, upon an Indictment of the aforesaid Court, had been convicted of the crime of conspiracy, with sundry other persons, unjustly and fraudulently to obtain of Etienne Drouin, divers large sums of money, the said Charles Baptiste Bouc be expelled this House.*

On the 24th of January, 1801, the same Resolution respecting Charles Baptiste Bouc, was adopted.†

On the 22nd March, 1802, it was

Resolved, That Charles Baptiste Bouc, a member for the County of Effingham, be expelled this House for the reasons set forth in the Resolutions of 2nd of April, 1800; and of the 24th of January, 1801; and that he be declared disqualified and incapable of sitting or voting as a member of this House, in this present Parliament.‡

CONTEMPT.

On the 17th of February, 1817, it was

Resolved, That Samuel Wentworth Monk, one of the Joint Prothonotaries for Montreal, has refused to exhibit certain records in his possession, at Quebec, which he was ordered to produce by the Special Committee appointed to investigate the charges against L. C. Foucher, Esq.

Resolved, That the said S. W. Monk has been guilty of a contempt of this House, and a violation of its privileges; that he be taken into the custody of the Sergeant-at-Arms, and that the Speaker do issue his warrant accordingly.

---

*Journals, 1800.   † Journals, 1801.   ‡ Journals, 1802.

On the 22nd of February, 1817, the Speaker informed the House that he had signed the warrant for the committment of Mr. Monk to the Quebec gaol. The Deputy-Sergeant-at-Arms at the Bar then acquainted the House that he held the Gaoler's receipt for the body of Mr. Monk.*

The Parliament of Quebec was prorogued on the 22nd day of March, 1817, and, on that day the Court—then sitting for the trial of crimes and criminal offences—on motion, granted a writ of *habeas corpus*, and the above cause of detention being returnable, it was moved that Samuel Wentworth Monk be discharged. The Court, without determining whether the detention of Mr. Monk was legal or illegal, whether the warrant by which he was detained was accurate or inaccurate, discharged him upon the ground that the period for which he was committed had expired. †

FALSE EVIDENCE.

On the 25th of February, 1817, Janvier D. Lacroix was, on the Speaker's warrant, committed to the Quebec gaol for "a high misdemeanour and a breach of the privileges of the House," in having, in his examination before a Special Committee, "wilfully and maliciously given false evidence." ‡

PRIVILEGE IN THE LEGISLATIVE COUNCIL OF LOWER CANADA.

But it was not in the case of the popular and elective

---

* Journals, 1817. † Stuart's L. C. R., pp. 120-121. ‡ Journals, 1817.

branch of the Legislature alone that the Canadian Judiciary, in times past, admitted and confirmed the claims for Privileges. In the case of *Daniel Tracy*, reported in Stuart, L. C. R., pp. 478–517, the Court held that "the Legislative Council has a right to commit, for breach of Privilege or in cases of libel; and the Court will not notice any defect in the warrant of commitment for such an offence after conviction." The libel was published in the *Montreal Vindicator* of the 3rd January, 1832.

The same order was entered in the case of *Ludger Duvernay*, brought before the Court by another writ of *habeas corpus*, upon a conviction by the Legislative Council on the 17th of January, 1832, for a similar breach of Privilege, in publishing in the paper, *La Minerve*, on the 9th January, 1831, a libel upon that branch of the Legislature. Justice Kerr, in the course of his remarks, observed: "But it has been argued by the defendant's advocate, that the Legislative Council has acquired no such power (that of the House of Lords, in the matter of Privilege), by immemorial custom and usage, and that the Parliamentary Charter of the year 1791 confers no such authority upon it. I certainly admit that this body does not possess, like the House of Lords, a right to fine and imprison beyond the Session, nor so extensive Privileges as the Lords and Commons possess. But can the exercise of the power of proceeding summarily and committing for a libel against the Legislative Council, as an aggregate body, be refused to them without their sinking into utter contempt and inefficiency ?

. . . "And whether a political institution is vested with the authority to make laws, or to explain and enforce them, it must of necessity possess all the powers requisite to ensure the purposes for which it was created. . . . The counsel for the defendants appear to consider the Privileges of both Houses of Parliament, of punishing for contempt, to be derived from the *Aula Regis*, which exercised all the authority of a Supreme Court of Justice; but the Ecclesiastical and Admiralty Courts, which do not derive their jurisdiction from the same source, exercise the same right of punishing summarily all contempts committed against their dignity and authority."

Justice Bowen, in pronouncing his decision said amongst other things: "Looking at the Act, 31 Geo. III., cap. 31, we find that the Provincial Legislature is empowered 'to make laws for the peace, welfare, and good government of the Province;' and in no part of this Act is there any mention of what shall be the Privileges of either branch of the Provincial Legislature; but it is certainly true that the framers of it intended to confer upon the Provinces of Upper and Lower Canada, a Constitution modelled, as far as circumstances would permit, precisely upon that of Great Britain. It has been well observed by Sir William Blackstone, treating upon this very subject, "that the Privileges of Parliament are large and indefinite; that if all the Privileges of Parliament were once to be set down and *ascertained*, and no Privilege to be allowed but what was so defined and determined, it were easy for the Executive Power to devise some new case, not within the line of Privilege, and *under pretence thereof*, to harass any refractory member and violate the freedom of Parliament;' the dignity and independence of the two Houses are therefore, in great measure, preserved by keeping their privileges *indefinite*. . . . .

"Besides, by the conviction before us, the Legislative Council have done no more than the House of Commons has invariably done upon similar occasions—imprisoned the offender during the Session of the Legislature, and in doing so have exercised a power which, during a period of nearly forty years, has been frequently exercised by the Assembly of this Province. . . . That these Privileges have likewise been acted upon by other Provincial Legislatures, and have been recognized by the highest authority, may be seen by the Journals of the Assembly of Jamaica, in 1808, in the case of Major-General Carmichael. . . . .

"This Province enjoys a Constitution similar to that of England, in virtue of a particular Statute, it is true, to make laws for the welfare and good government of the Province. Although the Statute mentions only this power, it does not deprive the Colonial Legislatures of their powers which are inherent and necessary for bodies constituted to perform their duties with liberty, independence, and for the general good. . . . . If in England this power is recognised as inherent in the Constitution, that is to say, as a Parliamentary law, necessary to the independence of their bodies, as a law of the country, it exists in this country. In granting us the

Constitution, Great Britain has given us the laws to protect it. Although the Constitutional Act maintains but certain particular duties, this does not deprive the Colonial Legislature of other powers which are enjoyed by the other Colonies, where Constitutions are only established by Charter; indeed the Provincial Legislature has performed other duties inherent to the Imperial Parliament, and the right of doing which cannot be denied to our Provincial Legislature, although not mentioned in the Constitutional Acts; and *their duties are also of high importance, and required power and independence of a Constitutional character to fulfil them. These rights have been claimed and exercised in this country since the commencement of the Constitution.*"*

We have now done with the illustrations of the supported claims of the Provincial Legislatures of Upper and Lower Canada. Enough has been brought forward to prove that they were not mere automata, created by the Constitutional and Union Acts, and gyrating in aimless impotence in the narrow circles of a statute law. Proof has been given that these old Legislatures were something nobler and more powerful than the mere letter of the Acts which gave them a legal and technical blaim to exist. Our Canadian Courts, always and righteously jealous of the least infringement of personal liberty, felt bound, even when that liberty was jeopardised in conflict with these Legislatures, to recognise that, in certain cases they possessed powers inherent, and independent of the phrase-

---

* The italics in the foregoing are in the Report.

ology of the statute-draftsman. In a word, the Canadian tribunals ruled that, barring those sovereign attributes which belong, by assured and pre-eminent right, to the Imperial Legislature, and which cannot be delegated, the Legislatures of the Provinces of Upper, Lower, and United Canada were not mere deliberative bodies with an incidental permission to enact laws, but were real and veritable Parliaments.

CHAPTER VI.

PRIVILEGE IN THE LATE PROVINCE OF CANADA.

NOW for a few illustrations of the manner in which the Parliament of the late Province of Canada asserted and vindicated its privileges, in its endeavours "to make laws for the peace, welfare and good government" of the country."

In re the Argenteuil Election.—D. G. Lebel, Deputy Returning Officer for St. Hermas, was summoned before the Bar of the House, to give an account of his conduct at the said election. Leave was given him to produce witnesses. He was declared guilty of a breach of Privilege in closing the poll several hours before the time prescribed by law, without any adequate reason therefor, and was committed to gaol for twenty-four hours.[*]

---

[*] Journals, 1854-5.

Mr. T. Brodeur, member for Bagot, refused to obey the order of the House, which directed him to be examined as returning officer, touching the Bagot election. He was taken into custody and placed at the Bar, but having answered the questions put to him by the House, was discharged.*

A peculiar case was that of Mr. J. Gleason, because the House took cognizance of a matter that was an offence at law. For his conduct in sending a challenge to Mr. N. Casault, M.P.P., a member of the Bellechasse Election Committee, Mr. Gleason was placed at the Bar; but on his petition expressing his sorrow and praying the indulgence of the House, he was discharged from custody.†

In re the Lotbinière Election of 1858. James McCullough, for having disobeyed the order of the House to attend and give evidence touching the election for the County of Lotbiniere (1858), was placed at the Bar. He was examined. Motion that J. McCullough, Poll Clerk, and George Cote, Deputy Returning Officer, for the Parish of St. Sylvestre, are guilty of a gross fraud and breach of Privilege in being privy to the fraudulent registration on the poll-book of fictitious names, etc. Both were found guilty and committed to gaol during pleasure. Cote was discharged on May 12th, but McCullough was kept in prison until the 6th of August, 1858, when he was liberated by the Speaker's warrant, directed to the keeper of the common gaol of York and Peel.‡

The next case in point is the Saguenay Election. M.

---

* Journals, 1854-5.   † *Ibid.*   ‡ Journals, 1858.

McCarty, A. Guay, L. Lavoie, and E. Tremblay appeared at the Bar to answer for their conduct at the election. They were severally found guilty of a breach of Privilege, having been privy to the fraudulent inscribing of names on the poll-books for the parishes for which they were respectively Deputy Returning Officers, and were committed to gaol for ten days. The Speaker reported that an application had been made to the Courts, on the part of Lavoie, for a writ of *Habeas Corpus.**

The case of *Lavoie*, was one which during the existence of the Parliament of the late Province of Canada, was contested before the courts.

"Lavoie was committed to gaol by the House of Assembly of the Province of Canada, on the warrant of the Speaker of the House, for the space of ten days, for breach of the Privileges of the House, in that, as Deputy Returning Officer, he had connived at and been guilty of gross fraud," etc.

"The court held, on his petition for a writ of *Habeas Corpus*, that such malversation of office was a breach of the Privileges of the House, and that the House had in such case the power of determining judicially all matters touching the election of its own members, including the performance of the duty of those officers who are entrusted with the regulation of the election of its members; and further, that the Courts of Law could not inquire under such a commitment, nor discharge nor bail a person so committed; yet, as the commitment did not

---

* Journals, 1854-5.

profess to be for contempt, but was evidently arbitrary, unjust, etc., the court would not only be competent, but bound to discharge the person." *

CHAPTER VII.

FEDERAL AND PROVINCIAL POWERS COMPARED.

IT is now in order to consider in brief—
 1. The powers given to the Dominion and to the Provinces of Ontario and Quebec by the British North American Act.

 2. The powers with which the Legislatures of these two Provinces have clothed themselves, in order to carry out the purposes for which they exist.

 3. The opinion of the Tribunals on the powers of the Provincial Parliaments, those inherited and those conferred.

 4. The difference between the powers of the Imperial and the Federal Parliaments.

Section 90 of the British North American Act thus defines some of the powers conferred on the Provincial Legislatures :—

"The following provisions of this Act respecting the Parliament of Canada—namely: the Provisions relating to Appropriation and Tax Bills, the Recommendation of

---

* Stephens' Quebec Law Digest, pp. 922-923.

Money Votes, the Assent to Bills, the Disallowance of Acts, and the Signification of pleasure on Bills Reserved —shall extend and apply to the Legislatures of the several Provinces, as if those Provisions were here re-enacted and made applicable in terms to the respective Provinces and the Legislatures thereof, with the substitution of the Lieutenant-Governor of the Province for the Governor-General, of the Governor-General for the Queen, and for a Secretary of State, of one year for two years,* and of the Province for Canada."

No argument is needed to prove that the powers conferred on the Provinces by this 90th section, are amongst the most important that justify the existence of a Parliament. The Provincial Legislatures are made the participants of the Federal Parliament, " as if these provisions were here re-enacted " in the power to deal with the people's money; a right which, entrusted for the time being, by the people to their responsible representatives, lies at the root of Parliamentary Government and Free Institutions.

The latter part of the section shows that the powers conferred are part of those exercised by the late Parliament of Canada, and are transmitted unimpaired to the Provincial Legislatures.

It is but right to admit, that the Federal Parliament is

---

* This refers to the period—one year—within which, and not after, the Governor-General has authority to disallow Provincial Legislation. During the existence of the late Province of Canada two years was the period within which the Imperial authorities could exercise the veto.

in possession of larger powers than the Provincial Legislatures. But it may be possible to show that these powers differ more in degree than they do in kind. In attempting to make this comparative similarity apparent, there is no desire to belittle the Parliament of Canada. Such as it is, that Legislature is our own; it represents, in a tentative way, the idea of Nationhood. It is a formative power, shaping out of scattered materials something that shall be the embodiment of a compact but individualized National life; something less than the British Empire, but greater than a Province.

Section 91 of the British North America Act deals with the "Distribution of Legislative powers." Under the heading "Powers of Parliament," there are enumerated twenty-eight subjects reserved to the Federal Legislature.

Section 92 of the Act enumerates the subjects under the control of the Provincial Legislatures: they are sixteen in number.

For the purposes of comparison, the more important of the subjects reserved to each Legislature will be placed side by side, not in numerical procession, as in the Act, but according to relationship.

FEDERAL POWERS.	PROVINCIAL POWERS.
3. The raising of money by any mode or system of taxation.	2. Direct Taxation within the Province, in order to the raising of a Revenue for Provincial purposes.
4. The borrowing of money on the public credit.	3. Borrowing money on the sole credit of the Province.
8. The fixing of and providing for the salaries and allowances of Civil and other officers of the Government of Canada.	4. The establishment and tenure of Provincial offices and the appointment and payment of Provincial officers.

FEDERAL POWERS—(*Continued*).

11. Quarantine and the establishment and maintenance of Marine Hospitals.

24. Indians, and lands reserved for the Indians.

26. Marriage and Divorce.

27. The Criminal Law except the Constitution of the Courts of Criminal Jurisdiction, but including the procedure in Criminal matters.

28. The Establishment, Maintenance and Management of Penitentiaries.

PROVINCIAL POWERS—(*Continued*).

7. The establishment, maintenance, and management of Hospitals, Asylums, Charities and Eleemosynary Institutions in and for the Province, other than Marine Hospitals.

5. The management and sale of the Public Lands belonging to the Province, and of the Timber and Wood Thereon.

12. The Solemnization of Marriage in the Province.

14. The Administration of Justice in the Province, including the Constitution, Maintenance, and Organization of Provincial Courts, both of Civil and Criminal Jurisdiction, and including Procedure in Civil matters in those Courts.

6. The Establishment, Maintenance, and Management of Public and Reformatory Prisons in and for the Province.

The following are the more important of the remaining Federal and Provincial Powers not placed in comparison above :—

(Reserved for the Federal Parliament :)
The Regulation of Trade and Commerce.
Postal Service.
Militia, Military, and Naval Service and Defence.
Navigation and Shipping.
Currency and Coinage,
Banking, Incorporation of Banks, and the issue of paper money.
Bankruptcy and Insolvency.
(Reserved for the Provincial Legislatures :)
The Amendment from time to time, notwithstanding

anything in this Act, of the Constitution of the Province, except as regards the Office of Lieutenant-Governor.

Municipal Institutions in the Province.

Local Works snd undertakings, other than such as are excepted in sub-section 10.

The Incorporation of Companies with Provincial Objects.

Property aud Civil rights in the Province.

Education.

It will be seen from the comparison of Federal and Provincial powers, given above, that there exists the closest relationship between between them, and that there is no transcendant superiority vested in the Dominion Parliament.

As regards the internal and material interests of each of the Provinces, their municipal self-government, their systems of education, their public lands and their development, and the administration of justice, the Local Legislatures are of much greater importance than the Federal Parliament. Over those vital and complex functions of a free Commonwealth, which are known as Civil Rights and which are the life and marrow of local Self-Government and Constitutional citizenship, the Provincial Parliaments rule supreme.

It must be borne in mind that the Federal Parliament is the offspring of the Provincial Legislatures; that it is not their progenitor; and that in confiding to it such of their powers as were necessary to establish it as a greater

Representative Institution than themselves, there were yet certain powers which they reserved for their own behoof.

As an illustration of these reserved powers, may be cited the last clause of Section 94 of the British North America Act. The section is headed " Uniformity of Laws in Ontario, Nova Scotia, and New Brunswick." This uniformity has reference to "all or any of the laws relative to property and civil rights" in the three Provinces just named, and to the procedure " of all or any of the Courts in those three Provinces." But the last clause of this section declares that "any Act of the Parliament of Canada making provision for such uniformity shall not have effect in any Province unless and until it is adopted and enacted by the Legislature thereof."

In the framing of the British North America Act great care was taken to avoid making violent alterations in the distinctive Institutions of some of the Provinces which were parties to the Federal compact. The French system of jurisprudence in Lower Canada was left inviolate. Although "Marriage and Divorce" are subjects placed specially under Federal control, yet no hand was laid on the Court of Divorce and Matrimonial Causes, which then existed in New Brunswick, and which still exercises its functions in that Province.

In one respect the Provincial Legislatures have a pre-eminent advantage over the Federal Parliament: they can at any time amend the Constitution, except as regards the office of Lieutenant-Governor. But even this power would not be denied by the Imperial Government, if we may judge from a reference to Colonial Governors, in a speech delivered by the Right Hon. W. E. Gladstone, in the House of Commons, on March 22, 1867, on the subject of the Canada Loan Bill, Mr Gladstone said:

"We have for a full quarter of a century acknowledged absolutely the right of self-Government in the colonies. We do not expect the laws of Canada or of Australia to be modelled according to our own ideas. We grant them a greater freedom from interference than, as amongst the three kingdoms, the Legislatures grants to the peculiar ideas that may happen to prevail in one of those three. We have carried it to this point, that as far as regards the Administration, I believe it may be said that the only officer appointed by the Colonial Secretary is the Governor; and I believe there cannot be a doubt that if it were the well-ascertained desire of the Colonies to have the appointment of their own Governor, the Imperial Parliament would at once make over to them that power."*

---

* *Hansard*, vol. 186, p. 753.

CHAPTER VIII.

SIR JOHN A. MACDONALD'S ORIGINAL MEMORANDUM ON DISALLOWANCE OF PROVINCIAL ACTS.

THE new system of Confederation had scarcely begun to work, when it became necessary to provide against the expected clashing of Federal and Provincial interests.

Accordingly, on the 8th of June, 1868, Sir John Macdonald, the Minister of Justice, prepared a memorandum on the subject of the powers of disallowance of the Acts of the Local Legislatures, possessed by the Federal Government.* It is in part as follows:

"The undersigned begs to submit for the consideration of Your Excellency, that it is expedient to settle the course to be pursued with respect to the Acts passed by the Provincial Legislatures.

"In deciding whether any Acts of a Provincial Legislature should be disallowed or sanctioned, the Government must not only consider whether it affects the interest of the whole Dominion or not; but also, whether it be unconstitutional, whether it exceeds the jurisdiction conferred on Local Legislatures, and, in cases where the jurisdiction is concurrent, whether it clashes with the Legislation of the General Parliament.

---

* Sessional Papers of Canada, 1869, No. 18.

" As it is of importance that the course of Local Legislation should be interferred with as little as possible, and the power of disallowance exercised with great caution, and only in cases where the law and the general interests of the Dominion imperatively demand it, the undersigned recommends that the following course be pursued :—

"That, on receipt by Your Excellency, of the Acts passed in any Province, they be referred to the Minister of Justice for report, and that he, with all convenient speed do report as to those Acts which he considers free from objection of any kind ; and, if such report be approved by Your Excellency in Council, that such approval be forthwith communicated to the Provincial Government.

" That he make a separate report, or separate reports, on those Acts which he may consider :—

" 1. As being altegether illegal or unconstitutional ;

" 2. As illegal or unconstitutional in part.

" 3. In cases of concurrent jurisdiction as clashing with the Legislation of the general Parliament ;

"4. As affecting the interests of the Dominion generally;

" And that in such report or reports, he gives his reasons for his opinions.

"That, where a measure is considered only partially defective, or where objectionable, as being prejudicial to the general interests of the Dominion, or as clashing with its Legislation, communication should be had with the Provincial Government with respect to such measure, and that, in such case, the Act should not be disallowed, if the general interests permit such a course, until the Local

Government has an opportunity of considering and discussing the objections taken, and the Local Legislatures has also an opportunity of remedying the defects found to exist."

The memorandum was approved by the Governor-General in Council, on the 9th of June, 1868; on the 11th of the same month it was transmitted to the Lieutenant-Governors of the Provinces of Ontario, Quebec, Nova Scotia and New Brunswick.* The memorandum approaches the subject of the disallowance of Provincial legislation, in a manner that is at once statesmanlike and liberal. It furnishes the key to the interpretation to be placed by all Ministers of Justice on questions involving Federal and Provincial prerogatives in matters of law-making. Those who assume that the Parliament of Canada is, by right and by statute, placed high above the plane of Provincial Legislatures, will no doubt notice that, in two separate places in his memorandum, Sir John Macdonald admits that there are "cases where the jurisdiction is concurrent."

---

* In the communication of the Hon. Mr. Langevin, Secretary of State transmitting the memorandum, each Lieutenant-Governor is styled "Your Excellency."

CHAPTER IX.

PRIVILEGES OF THE ONTARIO LEGISLATURE: DISALLOWANCE OF THE ACT DEFINING THEM.

ON the 19th of December, 1868, the Lieutenant-Governor of Ontario assented to an Act " to define the Privileges, Immunities and Powers of the Legislative Assembly of that Province ;" 32 Vic., cap. 3.

The Act, in Section 1, declared that the privileges of the Legislative Assembly should be the same as those of the Commons House of Parliament of Canada. Section 2 provided that those privileges should be part of the Public and General Law of Ontario; that it should not be necessary to plead the same; but that all Courts and Judges of Ontario should take judicial notice of them.

The Act was referred to the Law Officers of the Crown in England to pronounce on its constitutionality.*

The Law Officers, in a communication to the Earl of Granville, Secretary of State for the Colonies, dated, Temple, 4th May, 1869, pronounced against the Act.

Sir John Macdonald, in a report dated 14th of July, 1869, advanced the propositions that follow in respect to the Act in question :—

"With reference to the following Act passed by the

---

* Sessional papers, Canada, 1877. No. 89, p. 202, *et seq.*

Legislature of the Province of Ontario at its second Session, 32 Victoria, the undersigned has the honour to report as follows :

"Chapter 3. That Chapter 3, intituled an 'Act to define the privileges, immunities and powers of the Legislative Assembly, and to give summary protection to persons employed in the publication of Sessional papers,' is objectionable.

"By the 18th clause of the British North America Act, 1867, it is enacted that the privileges, immunities and powers to be held, enjoyed and exercised by the Senate and by the House of Commons of the Dominion of Canada, shall be such as shall be from time to time defined by Act of the Parliament of Canada, but so that the same shall never exceed those held, enjoyed and exercised at the passing of such Act by the House of Commons of the United Kingdom.

"It is to be assumed that the power to pass an Act defining those privileges was conferred upon the Parliament of Canada on the ground that without such a provision the Parliament of Canada could not have passed any such Act.

"It is clear, from the current of judicial decision in England, that neither of the branches of a Colonial Legislature have any inherent right to the privileges of the Imperial Parliament. Perhaps, however, under the Legislative powers given to the Dominion by the 91st section of the Union Act, to make laws "for the peace, order, and good government of Canada," it might have passed an

Act without any enabling power from the paramount authority, establishing and defining the privileges of its two Chambers. However, this may be with respect to the General Parliament, it is to be observed that there is no clause in the Union Act similar to the 18th, giving to the Provincial Legislatures power to define or establish their privileges, and that no general powers of legislation for the good government of the Provinces are given to their Legislatures.

"Their powers are strictly limited to those conferred by the 92nd, 93rd, 94th and 95th clauses of the Union Act.

"By the Act in question it will be seen that the Legislature of Ontario has declared that the Legislative Assembly and its members shall enjoy the same privileges as those exercised by the House of Commons of Canada.

"It would seem, therefore, that this Act is in excess of the power of the Provincial Legislature. If it has any power to legislate in the matter at all, it seems to follow that while the General Parliament can, under the 18th clause, confer no greater privileges than those enjoyed by the Imperial House of Commons, the Provincial Legislature, being bound to no such limitation, might, if it were so disposed, confer upon itself and its members privileges in excess of those belonging to those of the House of Commons of England."

Honourable John Sandfield Macdonald, Premier of Ontario, replied to the Minister of Justice. In a copy of a Minute of Council, approved by "His Excellency," the

Lieutenant-Governor, the 21st of September, 1869, it is stated that "the Committee (of Council) concur in the report of the Honourable the Attorney-General, and in the reasons therein given for the constitutionality of the said Act, and advise that the same be approved of."

The Report of Attorney-General Macdonald, who had before him the opinions of the Law Officers of the Crown, as to the Acts being beyond the powers of the Ontario Legislature, was as follows:—

"The undersigned, to whom His Excellency the Lieutenant-Governor referred the letter of the under Secretary of State at Ottawa, dated the 24th day of July last, transmitting therewith certain reports and communications, and all bearing on specific objections to three several Acts passed during the last Session of the Ontario Legislature, has the honour to submit the following observations for His Excellency's consideration.

"With respect to Chapter 3, intituled an "Act to define tho privileges, immunities and powers of the Legislative Assembly, and to give summary protection to persons employed in the publication of Sessional Papers," it is said the powers of the Legislature of Ontario are strictly limited to those conferred by the 92, 93, 94 and 95 clauses of the Union ; Act that there is no general power conferred on the respective Local Legislatures to enact laws for the good government of the Provinces as there has been to the general or Dominion Legislature, and that the express provision contained in the 13th section of the Union Act, granting to the Senate and House of Commons of Canada, and to the members thereof respectively, " shall be such as are from time to time defined by the Act of the Parliament of Canada, but so that the same shall never exceed those at the passing of this Act held, enjoyed and exercised by the Commons House of Parliament of the United Kingdom of Great Britain and Ireland, and by the members thereof," shows that without such a provision the Parliament of Canada could not have passed such an Act. On these grounds it has been concluded that the Ontario Statute under consideration is in excess of the power of the Ontario Legislature.

"To justify this conclusion, it is said that if the Local Legislature can pass such a law because it is not trammelled, it may pass a law exceeding the limitation which has been placed on the Dominion Parliament by the 18th section of the Union Act.

"It may not be quite easy to define precisely what power the Local Legislature may or may not lawfully exercise on the very numerous subjects which are within its jurisdiction.

"It cannot be denied that the Legislature must possess the power, if not by mere regulation, by Statute at any rate, to provide for the orderly course of its proceedings —for freedom from arrest of its members whilst attending their duties, and for a reasonable time before and after each Session for freedom of speech, not only against the Crown, but against private persons, for the right to publish and distribute generally such matters as may be deemed conducive to the public interest, without the risk of suit for publishing what might be otherwise deemed to be defamatory, and for the punishment of all persons guilty of contempt in the face of the House, or before its Committees.

"For without such protection the Legislature would be unable to maintain its dignity, and would be more feeble than a Justice of the Peace who has a right to punish for contempt committed at his Petty Sessions.

"And it would be singular that a Legislative Body which can confer such privileges upon any Court or Municipal body should not be able to grant them to itself.

"The undersigned believes also that the Ontario Legislature could have gone beyond the privileges just named and could have declared that members of the Legislature should be proceeded against in civil suits by a particular kind of process, and that all suits against them should be tried in a particular court, or that no civil suit at all should be commenced or prosecuted against them during the Session of the House, or for a certain time before or after the Session.

"The undersigned is also of opinion that witnesses, summoned to attend before the House or a Committee, should be liable to be proceeded against by the House for contempt in disobeying the process, or in declining to give evidence or otherwise, and that all matters pertaining to the election of members should be tried and determined by the House.

"The only privileges which the House of Commons in England possesses which may not be considered as applicable here are, when it acts as the grand inquest of the nation, to inquire into grave offences, and when it accuses, for the purpose of a trial, for the offence found, and when it adjudicates upon and punishes contempts out of the House.

"Yet, the undersigned believes there is nothing to prevent the Legislature of Ontario from granting the power of inquisition to itself by Statute.

"It may, undoubtedly, withdraw the power from grand jurors by abolishing the grand jury system, or by transferring the powers now exercised by grand jurors to any other power, body or person.

"And that the Legislature may also grant to itself the power to try for and to punish contempts not committed before the House. It is familiar to every one acquainted with the practice of the Superior Courts, to what extent contempts to the process and officers of such Courts are punished, though not committed in the precincts of the Courts. There is no decision, the undersigned believes, at all touching the jurisdiction of the Legislature to pass a statute for such purposes, though there are decisions that a legislative body has, as such, no inherent right to assume such power. Powers analogous to those which are exercisable by the British House of Commons, because the latter body has acquired theirs by long usage and custom only, and powers so acquired are not assumable by other bodies possessing general legislative authority in other places.

"The Dominion Act contains nothing against the legislation in question.

"It does not declare that the Legislature of Ontario shall

have authority over those matters which are mentioned in the Act, but that it may exclusively make laws relating to those subjects therein enumerated.

"And it seems difficult to maintain that a Legislature which may amend the Constitution of the Province, and may legislate on property and civil rights, and generally on all matters af a mere local or private nature, may not by Statute provide that the like power which the House of Commons of the Dominion and the members thereof possess, may be possessed also by the Legislative Assembly of Ontario, and the representatives of the people assembled therein and elected thereto by the same constitutents who send Members to the Commons.

"The argument that the Legislature of Ontario may grant to the Assembly greater powers to the matters alluded to, because not restricted from doing so, than the House of Commons of Canada possesses, because it is restricted from assuming or exercising greater privileges than those which the British House of Commons enjoyed, is not in the opinion of the undersigned an answer to the exercise of those powers which are not more extensive than the House of Commons does possess.

"It does not follow that the Legislature of Ontario has the power to exercise greater authority than the House of Commons of Canada can exercise.

"The limitation placed by the Union Act upon the greater body must no doubt be held by just construction of the Statute to operate by limitation upon the subordinate Legislatures as well.

"The conclusion to which the undersigned has arrived with respect to the constitutionality of the Ontario Act 32 Vic., chap. 3, is that it is not liable to the exceptions, which have been taken to it, and that sufficient consideration has not, in his humble opinion, been given to the important distinction between powers claimed by the authority of a Statute and powers claimed as inherently belonging to a Legislative body."

On the 23rd of October, 1869, a memorandum, by Sir John A. Macdonald, recommending the disallowance of the Act was approved of by the Governor-General in Council, and a copy of it ordered to be transmitted to the Lieutenant-Governor of Ontario.

A despatch from Hon. Mr. Langevin, Secretary of State, to Lieutenant-Governor Howland, dated 26 October, 1869, transmitted the foregoing memorandum. The despatch proceeds:—

"May I request you to give me timely notice, for His Excellency's information, of the course proposed to be adopted by your advisers with regard to the three Acts under consideration."

The Parliament of Ontario met on the 3rd of November, 1869. But Hon. John Sandfield Macdonald gave no indication of yielding; he gave "no timely notice;" he submitted no motion for the repeal of the Act. He was not to be convinced, either by the opinions of the Law Officers of the Crown, or by the arguments of the Minister of Justice, that this Statute was beyond the powers of the Ontario Legislature.

The Act 32 vic., cap. 3, "To define the Privileges, Immunities and Powers of the Legislative Assembly," was disallowed by proclamation in the Canada *Gazette* of the 4th December, 1869.

CHAPTER X.

PRIVILEGES OF THE LEGISLATURE OF QUEBEC: DISALLOWANCE.

ON the 5th of April, 1869, An Act "To define the Privileges, Immunities and Powers of the Legislative Council and Legislative Assembly of Quebec," received the assent of the Lieutenant-Governor of that Province: (32 Vic., cap. 4.)

Section 1 of the Act provided that the Privileges of the Legislative Council should be the same as those of the Senate of Canada. The language of sec. 1, 2 and 3, was similar to that in secs. 1 and 2 of the Ontario Statute.

In a memorandum dated 24th November, 1869, the Minister of Justice gave it as his opinion that it was not competent for the Quebec Legislature to pass the Act in question.

On the 26th November, 1869, the Governor in Council, declared his disallowance of the Act.*

But on the 1st of February, 1870, the following Act of the

---

* S. P. Canada, 1870. No. 35.

Quebec Legislature received the assent of the Lieutenant-Governor :—

"An Act to uphold the authority and dignity of the House of the Quebec Legislature, and the independence of the members thereof, and to protect persons publishing Parliamentary Papers."

The Act is also known as 33 Vic., cap. 5; and as "The Quebec Parliamentary Act."

The Quebec Act contains thirteen Sections; the Ontario Act which is noticed further on, twenty-one. Both Statutes, however, are practically the same in respect to the power to compel attendance of witnesses, and the production of papers; and the protection of persons acting under the authority of the Legislature.

The matters declared to be infringements of the Acts, such as assaults upon members, threatening them, or offering them bribes, tampering with witnesses and falsifying documents, are the same in both Satutes. Similar, also, are the enactments respecting freedom of speech, freedom from arrest, and exemption from jury service. Each Legislature takes upon itself the power to punish infringement of the Statutes in question.

But, in some respects the Acts differ. The 11th Section of the Ontario Statute provides that the "Assembly shall have all the rights and privileges of a Court of Record," etc. This has no counterpart in the Quebec Act. Sub-section 7, of Section 11 of the Ontario Act, makes disobedience to subpœnas or warrants an offence; Section 13 provides that any person declared "guilty of a contempt," shall be committed on the Speaker's warrant to the common gaol.

The Quebec Act is silent as to the punishment for disobedience of the Speaker's warrant; neither does it define, with the precision of the Ontario Statute, by what means the Legislature may order imprisonment.

This Act was allowed to go into operation without Federal interference.

CHAPTER XI.

THE LEGISLATURE OF ONTARIO AGAIN ASSERTS ITS PRIVILEGES.

ON the 10th of February, 1876, the Lieutenant-Governor of Ontario gave assent to "An Act respecting the Legislative Assembly." The powers devolving upon the Parliament of Ontario, by virtue of this Act are at once various and extensive.

It is not possible, in this place, to do more than glance, briefly, at the provisions of this Statute, which is known as 39 Vic. cap. 9. It is to be found at length in the Statutes of Ontario, 1875-76, and forms chapter 12 of the Consolidated Statutes of that Province.

Section 1 of this Act provides that the Legislative Assembly may, at all times, command and compel the attendance of witnesses before itself or any of its committees. The same rule applies to the production of papers.

Section 2 authorises the Speaker to issue his warrant or subpœna, requiring the attendance of persons, and the production of papers before the House, or any of its Committees.

Section 3 enacts that no person shall be liable, in damages, for any act done under the authority of the Legislative Assembly, and within its legal powers; that the warrants of the House may command the aid of all sheriffs, bailiffs, etc.

Section 4 assures to members freedom of speech and action in the Assembly.

Section 5 exempts members from arrest for any debt or cause of a civil nature, during any Session of the Legislature, or during the twenty days following, such Session.

Section 6 declares that during the periods mentioned in the preceding section, all members of the Assembly, all its officers, and all witnesses summoned before it or any of its committees, shall be exempt from serving as jurors in any court in this Province.

. . . .

Section 11 enacts that the Assembly shall have all the rights and privileges of a Court of Record, for the purpose of summarily enquiring into and punishing, as breaches of privilege, or as contempt of Court—without prejudice to the liability of the offenders to prosecution and punishment, criminally or otherwise, according to law, independently of this Act—the acts, matters and things following :—

1. Assaults, insults or libels upon members during the Session of the Legislature, and twenty days before and after the same.

2. Obstructing, threatening or attempting to force or intimidate members.

3. The offering to, or acceptance of, a bribe by any member to influence him in his proceedings as such, etc.

4. Assaults upon or interference with officers of the Assembly.

5. Tampering with any witness.

6. Giving false evidence, or refusing to give evidence or produce papers.

7. Disobedience to subpœnas or warrants.

8. Presenting to the Assembly or to any Committee thereof, any forged or falsified documents.

9. Forging or falsifying any of the records of the Assembly, or of its Committees, or any petition, etc.

10. Bringing action against a member, or causing his arrest, for anything done by him in the House as a member.

11. Effecting the arrest of a member for debt or cause of a civil nature, during a Session of a House, or during the twenty days preceding or the twenty days following such Session.

The Assembly is declared to possess all such powers and jurisdiction as may be necessary for inquiring into, judging and pronouncing upon the commir ion of any such acts, and awarding and carrying into execution the punishment thereof provided for by this Statute.

Section 12 provides that every person, for any of the offences enumerated above, in addition to any other punishment to which he may by law be subject, shall be liable to imprisonment, for such time during the Legislative Session then holding as the Assembly may determine.

Section 13 enacts that whenever the House finds any person guilty of a contempt for any of the acts, matters and things in section 11 set forth, and directs him to be imprisoned, the Speaker shall issue his warrant to the Sergeant-at-Arms or to the Keeper of the Common Jail to take such person into custody, and to detain him, in accordance with the order of the Legislative Assembly..

Section 14. The determination of the Legislative Assembly, upon any proceeding under this Act, and within the Legislative authority of this Province, shall be final and conclusive.

CHAPTER XII.

ONTARIO INTERFERES IN FEDERAL LEGISLATION.

THE Ontario House, at an early period of its existence, took a bold constitutional stand against the legislation of the Federal Parliament. The action was in defence of the Federal compact, and in vindication of the rights of the Provinces which were consenting parties to that Instrument.

On the 22rd November, 1869, the Honourable Edward Blake, eminent even then, in the dawn of his political career, for a lofty and impartial statemanship—a statesmanship which, since then, has been brightening and widening with the years—proposed a series of resolutions, condemning in the Federal Legislature, the breach of the terms of Confederation. This breach, in respect to Nova Scotia, " making altogether an alteration in favour of that Province of over $2,000,000, of which Ontario pays over $1,100,000,"

The Legislature of Ontario, by an overwhelming majority—64 to 12—

Resolved—"That, in the opinion of this House, the interests of the country requires such legislation as may remove all colour for the assumption by the Parliament of Canada of the power to disturb the financial relations established by the Union Act as between Canada and the several Provinces.

Here was early, energetic, and practical assertion of the rights of the Provinces, when the Federal Parliament was threatening the Federal Compact. Here was substantial interference in Dominion Legislation; and who is bold enough to say that this interference did not help to anchor the Federal ship of state, before she began to plunge and drift towards the breakers of bankruptcy ?

CHAPTER XIII.

THE QUEBEC JUDICIARY PRONOUNCES ON PROVINCIAL PRIVILEGES.

THE powers of the Provincial Legislatures as defined by the tribunals.

A test case was that of Mr. C. A. Dansereau, who was arrested on the warrant of the Speaker of the Quebec Legislative Assembly for refusing to give evidence in an inquiry concerning what was known as the " Tanneries Land Swap."

On the 17th of February, 1875, in Montreal, the petition of Mr. Dansereau for a writ of *habeas corpus* came before the judges of the Queen's Bench, in appeal. Chief Justice Dorion, Mr. Justice Taschereau, Mr Justice Sanborn and Mr Justice Monk agreed in refusing the petition ; Mr Justice Ramsay dissenting.

It is to be regretted that space compels the omission of the important observations of the learned Judges, with the exception of some of those of Mr. Justice Ramsay and Mr. Justice Sanborn.

The Court held—

"That the Legislative Assembly of the Province of Quebec has power to compel the attendance of witnesses before it, and may order a witness to be taken into custody by the Serjeant-at-Arms if he refuses to attend when summoned.

"The omission to state in the Speaker's Warrant of Arrest the grounds and reasons therefor, is not a fatal defect.

"The Quebec Statute 33 Vic. cap. 5, is within the powers of the Local Legislature."

Mr. Justice Ramsay (dissentient), in pronouncing against the power of the Speaker to order the arrest of Dansereau said, amongst other things:

"The last question, and the most important, is the warrant of attachment. . . A general warrant, which is nothing more than an order to the Serjeant-at-Arms to arrest A. or B., without expressing any cause whatever, cannot be justified on necessity by the most obsequious defender of arbitrary power. . ., The consequence of granting it is to give the Local Houses, respectively, unlimited authority over the persons and property of Her Majesty's subjects. . . For my part I have no hesitation about the illegality of general warrants. . . I must resist them morally with all the arguments I can command, materially with all the authority I may possess. I hold that they are unknown to the law, and that the precedents cannot legalise them. . . The power to issue a general warrant is given by no Statute to the Commons of England : by Section 18, B. N. A. Act, it is refused to the Houses of Parliament of Canada, and it is denied to all persons by many Statutes in express terms." (See the Petition of Rights, and 16 Charles 1, cap. 10.)

Mr. Justice Sanborn, in giving his decision, said, in part :
"The British North America Act of 1867 was enacted in response to the petition of the late Provinces of Canada, Nova Scotia, and New Brunswick, as stated in the preamble of the Act, ' to be federally united into one Dominion under the Crown of the United Kingdom of great Britain and Ireland, with a Constitution similar in principle to that of the United Kingdom.'

"The powers of Legislation and Representative Government, or as it has commonly been called, Responsible Government, were not new in Canada. They had been conceded to Canada, and exercised in their largest sense, from the time of the Union Act of 1840, and, in a somewhat more restricted sense, from the Act of 1791 to 1840. The late Province of Lower Canada was constituted a separate Province by the Act of 1791, with a Governor, a Legislative Council, and a Legislative Assembly, and it has never lost its identity. It had a separate body of laws, both as respacts Statute and Common Law, in civil matters. No powers that had been conceded were intended to be taken away by the British North America Act of 1867, and none, in fact, were taken away ; as it is not the wont of the British Government to withdraw Constitutional franchises once conceded.

"This Act, according to my understanding of it, distributed powers already existing, to be exercised within their prescribed limits, to different Legislatures constituting one Central Legislature and several subordinate ones, all upon the same model; without destroying the autonomy of the Provinces, or breaking the continuity of the prescriptive rights and traditions, of the respective Provinces. In a certain sense the powers of the Federal Parliament were derived from the Provinces, subject, of course, to the whole being a Colonial Dependency of the British Crown.

"The Provinces of Quebec and Ontario are, by the Sixth Section of the Act, declared to be the same that formerly comprised Upper and Lower Canada. This recognizes their previous existence prior to the Union Act of 1840. All through the Act these Provinces are recognized as having a previous existence and a constitutional history upon which the new fabric is based. Their laws remain unchanged, and the Constitution is preserved. The offices are the same in name and duties, except as to the office of Lieutenant-Governor, which is placed in the same relation to the Province of Quebec that the late Governor General sustained in the late Province of Canada. I think that it would be a great mistake to ignore the past govermental powers conferred upon, and exercised in, the Province now called Quebec, in determining the nature and privileges of the Legislative Assembly of this Province.

"The remark is as common as it is erroneous, that the Legislatures of the Provinces are mere large Municipal Corporations. It is true that every Government is a Corporation, but every Municipal Corporation is not a Government. Consider the powers given exclusively to Provincial Legislatures. They have sole jurisdiction over education, property, and civil rights, administration of justice and municipal institutions in the Province; subjects which affect vitally the welfare of society. The very Court which enables us to determine the matter now under consideration, holds its existence by the will of the Provincial Legislature. No such powers were ever conferred upon mere Municipalities in the ordinary sense. They are subjects which, in all nations, are entrusted to the highest legislative power. Legislatures make laws; Municipal Corporations make by-laws.

"If these Legislative powers confided to Provincial Legislatures are not to be exercised in all their amplitude, with the incidents attaching to them, they can be exercised, by no other sovereign power, while our present Constitution exists. They have been conceded by the Imperial Parliament; and it claims no further right, as a rule, to legislate upon our local affairs; and the powers given exclusively to the Local Legislature necessarily exclude the jurisdiction of the Federal Legislature.

"Blackstone says : ' By sovereign power is meant that of the making of laws; for wheresoever that power resides, all others must conform to and be directed by it, whatever appearance the outward form and administration of the Government may put on. For it is at any time in the option of the Legislature to alter that form and administration by a new edict or rule, and to put the execution of the laws into whatever hands it pleases, by constituting one or a few or many executive magistrates and all powers of the State must obey the legislative power in the discharge of the several functions, or the Constitution is at an end.'

. . . .

"The Local Legislatures are not permitted to amend the Constitution as respects the office of Lieutenant-Governor. In Section 65 of the B. N. A. Act, the powers and functions of the Lieutenant-Governor are specially defined. This establishes that, in the view of the framers of that Act, the powers and functions of this branch of Parliament form part of the Constitution; and, consequently, the powers of the other branches are equally a part of the Constitution; and ability to amend the Constitution as respects the Houses of the Legislatures, includes power to determine their respective powers and immunities.

"The arrest of Mr. Dansereau, by virtue of the power conferred by this Act, (33 Vic., cap. 5), is, apart from the question of privilege, inherent in, and incident to, every Legislative body. I hold that, under this Statute, the Legislative Assembly of the Province of Quebec has a right to compel the attendance of Mr. Dansereau before the Bar of their House. Thus holding, it is unnecessary for the purposes of this case to discuss the question of privilege as a Common Law right.

. . . .

"I consider that the present Legislative Council and Legislative Assembly of Quebec have a right to invoke the usuages and precedents of these Houses existing prior to the B. N. A. Act of 1867, from 1791 to the date of that Act. There is the notable precedent of the British Parliament dating their privileges prior to the Commonwealth, and the fact that the Commons subsequent to the Commonwealth did not insist upon the right to examine witnesses on oath as one of their privileges, which was insisted upon by that body during the Commonwealth.

"Whatever powers and immunities attached to the Legislative Assembly of the late Province of Lower Canada and the Legislative Assembly of the Province of Canada, as were necessarily incident to them in the proper exercise of their functions as Legislative bodies, I consider attach to the Legislative Assembly of the present Province of Quebec. In considering the privileges necessarily incident to Colonial Legislatures, we can only apply the Constitution of the Parliament of the United Kingdom, where the analogy obtains.

"The Senate of the Dominion, or the Legislative Council of the Province, cannot claim the judicial powers of the House of Lords; and yet there are many judicial powers to be exercised in connection with Legislation, the depository of which must be somewhere. For example, jurisdiction over divorce is given to the Federal Parliament. It has been thought necessary to assume power to examine witnesses upon oath, and determine the matter judicially, though neither Houses had greater powers than the Commons House of the United Kingdom. It became a necessary incident to the powers conferred.

"The Legislative Assembly of our Province has not the mere nude power of legislation. It has, by implication, by usuage, and by a Constitution modelled upon the English House of Commons, also an inquisitorial power, to make itself acquainted, by means of Committees, of the needs of the Province, and the evils that exist in society, over which it has control, in order to legislate intelligently, and administer wisely.

"Any person who refuses to attend, upon the summons of the Legislative Assembly, to give evidence, is obstructing that body in the legitimate execution of its functions. I think, without reference to the Statute already quoted, there must be an inherent right, in the Legislative Assembly, to compel persons to attend before them, and give evidence.

"This principle, it appears to me, is conceded in the cases of Kielly *vs.* Carson, and Doyle and Falconer. In the former Baron Parke said: 'We feel no doubt that such Assembly has the right of protecting itself from all impediments to the due course of its proceedings. To the full extent of every measure which it may be necessary to adopt, to secure free exercise of their legislative functions, they are justified in acting upon the principle of the Common Law.' This was said with reference to a Legislative Assembly acting under a Crown Charter, in a minor Province, and assuredly it should apply with much greater force to this Province, which, for many years, has been governed under a Statutory Constitution, and upon usages conformable to the British Constitution.

"The cases of Tracey, Monk, and Duvernay in our early jurisprudence, and the recent case, *ex parte* Lavoie, sanction these privileges as inherent in our Provincial Legislative Council and Legislative Assembly; and I find them recognized in the late cases in the Privy Council. I see no reason in this advanced stage of our Parliamentary history and progress in all the material interests which give to a nation importance, why these powers should be denied to our Local Legislature. . . .

"This warrant discloses no contempt. It is simply an exercise of the powers of the Legislative Assembly to bring Mr. Dansereau before that body. If this warrant were issued solely on the ground of privilege, it would be difficult to sanction it in its vague terms, without the purpose being shown; but, by the 2nd and 9th Sections of 33 Vic., cap. 5,* such warrant is permissible.

"I consider that the arbitrary form of the order is objectionable, but I cannot say that it is illegal. . . . I think the *Habeas Corpus* should be quashed, and the Serjeant-at-Arms be left to execute his warrant."

---

*"An Act to uphold the authority and dignity of the Houses of the Quebec Legislature," etc.

CHAPTER XIV.

THE CONTINUITY OF THE PROVINCIAL POWERS.

IN the foregoing case of Mr. Dansereau, petitioning for a writ of *Habeas Corpus*,

Mr. Justice Monk, in giving judgment, said, in part :—

" I shall offer a few remarks upon the powers, privileges and functions which, as it seems to me, at all times since the first granting of a Legislature to the Colony, have been, and which now necessarily must be, inherit in that Body, independent of any precedent or any usuage. It is a principle of the Common Law that, where political or other such bodies are organized, and powers granted, all the means and authority necessary for the exercise of their functions are also impliedly conferred, though not expressly mentioned. It seems plain to my mind, that the House does possess from necessity, and by implied and inherent prerogative, independent of usuage or precedent, the powers claimed in the present instance. But if we hesitate in regard to this view of the subject, does there not exist a usage, a jurisprudence, so to speak, in matters relating to the powers of the Local Parliament of Quebec, which must go far to remove all doubt in reference to these powers, as claimed in the present instance ? . .
Precedents and decisions furnish proof, if such were want-

ing, of the existence for nearly a century, of the law, usuages or authority here contended for. All this looks very much like a 'Lex et Consuetudo Parliamenti.'

"It has been repeatedly said that there have been three separate fundamental and distinct breaches in the continuity, so to speak of our Constitution: one in 1838, one in 1841, and the last in 1867. . . As a matter of fact, our Constitution has undergone suspensions, changes, modifications, and withal, ooccasional restorations. I think it may be safely held that if these Parliamentary powers, usages and privileges ever did exist, and since they did exist, they never were, by these vicissitudes in our Constitutional history, modified or abrograted. Inasmuch as the Confederation Act, in this respect, has left us where we were—that is, independent, supreme within our own sphere of legislation, it cannot be said to have interfered with these laws and usages of Parliament, such as they existed in 1867.

"Thus, then, as I view this part of the case before us, the authority and inherent privileges of the House of Assembly have virtually continued, though occasionally in abeyance, through all the changes of our Constitution; and they exist in as full force as they did for a long time, and immediately previous to Confederation. I consider myself, therefore, bound by what I regard as an established usage, and I cannot in the face of all this decide that, for nearly a century, and up to the present day, the Legislature of this country has, in the instances adverted to, and which, in part, illustrate its history, been acting as a mob, perpetrating illegal acts, and guilty of flagrant tyranny, and violations of the law of the land.

"It is unnecessary to refer at length to the decisions of the highest tribunals in England in order to show that the view here taken as to the inherent authority of Parliament and the force of Parliamentary precedent and usage, even in subordinate Legislatures, such as ours, have been fully sustained. None of these cases, it is true, are exactly, in point; but the principles there laid down clearly show that our decision in this case, upholding the power and authority of the Local Legislature is in entire conformity with what has been there laid down as law.

"I am clearly of opinion that our Legislature had power to pass that law (33 Vic., cap. 5); it has not been disallowed ; it has been in force for years, and we are bound by it, and, being so bound, we need not appeal to any other authority or laws, in order to decide this matter. Thus, as it appears to me, upon the three grounds—1st, the inherent and necessarry powers of our Local Legislatures ; 2nd, the usage, precedents and decisions in relation to the powers of our Legislature for nearly a hundred years ; and partly under and in virtue of the clear and peremptory authority and requirements of positive laws, the 33rd Vic., cap. 5, and the Statute of the same year which authorizes the administration of oaths to witnesses examined before committees of the House; we are bound to quash this writ of *Habeas Corpus*, and so uphold, in so far as this case involves the prerogatives of our Parliament, the authority of the House."*

---

* Lower Canada Jurist, 1875 : pp. 210-248.

In respect to the powers of the Legislature of Quebec, it has been further decided by the Courts, that " the Legislature of Quebec has power to provide procedure for the enforcement of penal Statutes enacted within its powers, and such Statutes are not part of the criminal law as contemplated by the B. N. A. Act.

" The power conferred on the Legislature of Quebec by the B. N. A. Act to impose the penalty of fine or imprisonment, does not restrict the Legislature of Quebec to the exercise of only one of those modes of punishment at a time by any particular Act."*

CHAPTER XV.

LIMITATION OF THE POWERS OF FEDERAL AND LOCAL PARLIAMENTS.

LET us now see what is the difference between the powers of the Imperial and Federal Parliaments.

Section 18 of the British North America Act, in its original shape, stood thus :

" The privileges, immunities, and powers to be held, enjoyed and exercised by the Senate and by the House of Commons, and by the members thereof, respectively, shall be such as are from time to time defined by the Acts of the Parliament of Canada, but so that the same shall

---

*Stephen's Quebec Law Digest : p. 739.

never exceed those at the passing of the Act held, enjoyed and exercised by the Commons House of Parliament of Great Britain and Ireland."

It was not long before it was practically demonstrated that this clause tied the hands of the Federal Parliament. The experience occurred after the investigation upon oath into the circumstances of what was known as the 'Pacific Scandal.' For the purposes of that inquiry, the Parliament of Canada passed an Act, 36 Vic., cap. 1," to provide for the examination of witnesses on oath by Committees of the Senate and House of Commons, in certain cases." But the Act was disallowed by the Queen. The reasons, as stated in the despatch of the Earl of Kimberley to the Earl of Dufferin, dated 30th June, 1873, were:

"That the Act was *ultra vires* of the Colonial Legislature, as being contrary to the express terms of Section 18 of the British North America Act, 1867, and that the Canadian Parliament could not vest in themselves the power to administer oaths, that being a power which the House of Commons did not possess in 1867, when the Imperial Act was passed. The Law Officers also reported that the Queen should be advised to disallow the Act."

But the Legislature of Quebec, by the Act 32 Vic. cap. 6 (1869); and the Legislature of Ontario by 35 Vic. cap. 5 (1871-2), conferred on their respective committees the power to examine witnesses on oath. Thus, the Local Legislatures, in one of the most important incidents of law-making, the right of inquiry, invested themselves with powers that were refused to the Federal Parliament.

In order to limit and legalise the privileges of the Federal Parliament, Section 18 of the British North America Act was repealed, and, by an Imperial Statute 38 and 39 Vic., cap. 38 (1875), the following provision took its place :

"The privileges, immunities, and powers to be held, enjoyed, and exercised by the Senate and by the House of Commons, and by the members thereof, respectively, shall be such as are from time to time defined by Act of the Parliament of Canada.

"But so that any Act of the Parliament of Canada defining such privileges, immunities, and powers, shall not confer any privileges, immunities or powers exceeding those at the passing of such Act, held, enjoyed, and exercised by the Commons House of Parliament of the United Kingdom of Great Britain and Ireland, and by the members thereof."

This same Imperial Act, by its second section, gave validity to the Statute of Parliament of Canada, 31 Vic., cap. 24, (1866), intituled "An Act to provide for oaths to witnesses being administered in certain cases, for the purposes of either House of Parliament," from the date at which the Royal assent was given thereto by the Governor-General. The Canadian Act of 1872 was thus set aside for that of 1868; the latter being considered, perhaps, the less objectionable.

The Speaker of the British House of Commons, when after his election, he presents himself to the Queen for approbation, lays claim by humble petition," to all their ancient and undoubted rights and privileges—particularly to freedom of speech in debate; to freedom from arrest of their persons and servants; to free access to Her Majesty, when occasion shall require."

It is claimed by some who advocate the unqualified omnipotence of the Federal Parliament, that the privileges thus claimed by the Speaker of the British House of the Commons, appertain to the Canadian Legislature. They do belong to that Parliament; and belong equally to the Provincial Parliaments, substituting, in the one case, the Governor-General, and in the other case, the Lieut.-Governor, for Her Majesty.

The Speaker of the Ontario Parliament, after his election, addressing himself to the Lieut.-Governor, uses much the same form of words. Hon. Rupert M. Wells, Speaker of the last Parliament of Ontario, after his election to that office, on November 25th, 1875, in his address to the Lieut.-Governor, " humbly claims all their (the Legislature's) undoubted rights and privileges, especially that they may have freedom of speech in their debates, access to your person at all seasonable times, etc."

But there is an imperial meaning and a tremendous force behind these verbal forms, when used by the Speaker of the British House of Commons. This meaning and this force have no place in the addresses of the Speakers of our Canadian Parliaments. The fact is, that the British Speaker's address to the Queen leaves unenumerated those powers of that semi-omnipotent House, which isolate and divide it from all other Legislatures by a gulf that neither kings nor colonies dare overpass.

The powers which the new Section 18 of the British North America Act allows the Federal Parliament to assume, now or hereafter, are, in the nature of things, limited and provincial. There is not, in their nature, the least approach to sovereignty; they relate, mainly, to the regulation of the Parliamentary procedure, in the present, to its possible amendment, in the future; restricting this possible amendment so that it shall not move beyond the practice in the Imperial House of Commons.

Political imagination, in its most fervid and patriotic flights, would shrink from picturing the Imperial and the Federal Legislatures as the possessors of co-equal powers. Still, there may be a few who fancy that the British North America Act, while giving pre-eminence to the Ottawa House of Commons as respects the Provincial Parliaments, constitutes it, in a mysterious and an indefinite manner, the compeer of the Imperial Legislature. For better or for worse, they will never be compeers.

The Imperial Parliament can change the Succession; can refuse to pass the Mutiny Act, and the Act for the Manning of the Navy, and thus disband the Army and put the Fleet out of commission; can repeal the Statutes by which the Colonies exercise the right of self-government; can impeach a Minister; can overturn the British Constitution and create another in its stead. These things are all within the powers of the Imperial Legislature. Its sovereignty over every foot of the earth's surface, where the British standard floats, is supreme. The great restraining power is not want of authority, but common sense, and concession, without which Constitutional government would be impossible, and liberty be expounded, not by the statesman but by the soldier.

It needs no more than the few illustrations just furnished to show the inherent and irreconcilable difference between the Parliament of Great Britain and the Parliament of Canada.

The fact is, that our Federal Legislature, proud as we may be of it, is in reality nothing more than a larger Local Parliament. The powers of the Provincial Assemblies end with their boundaries; the powers of the Ottawa Legislature terminate at our shore line.

A fair understanding of the functions of our Canadian Parliaments is the key to the successful working of our present political system. The difficulties that seem to beset a practical and satisfactory definition of the limits of Federal and Provincial sovereignty are none too great for a patriotic Canadian Statesmanship to overcome. It is satisfactory to remember that, in the event of an unyielding dispute as to contested prerogatives, an ultimate appeal can be made to the Imperial authorities. These high arbitrators can have comparatively little trouble in rectifying a possible complication, when it is borne in mind that, although both the Federal and the Provincial Legislatures are free, neither of them is independent.

CHAPTER XVI.

THE "OMNIPOTENCE" OF THE FEDERAL PARLIAMENT DISPELLED.

HON. EDWARD BLAKE, on the 23rd day of November, 1869, when introducing his Resolutions respecting the Nova Scotia Subsidy, said, amongst other things :*

"Well, then, it is said that the Parliament of Canada is omnipotent. So it is, to use an expression which is paradoxical, only omnipotent within its sphere. In certain defined limits, it has quite absolute power; but if it acts beyond those limits, there is always some tribunal to which the party aggrieved can appeal. I say that the idea that the Acts of the Parliament of Canada can not, by some Constitutional means, be appealed against, or be brought under consideration, is utterly destructive of the liberties of what, until that determination shall be arrived at, I shall call a free people. (Cheers.) The Federal Constitution, which defines its powers, must provide expressly to prevent any act in excess of these powers; and there is no doubt that any Act of Parliament, whether of the Parliament of Canada or of this Legislature, can be considered by the Courts, not merely as to the meaning of it, but also as to the question whether it is within the powers of either Legislature to pass it. There is no doubt about that;

---

* Toronto *Globe*, 24th November, 1879.

for this very question, which we are discussing now,* could go before a Court of Justice, if it was a thing in which a private party had such an interest in it that he was liable to sue and be sued in respect to it. The Courts of this country would be able to, would be entitled to, would be bound to, inquire into the question whether the Parliament of Canada had or had not exceeded its powers; and, therefore, it is quite ridiculous to say that the Parliament of Canada is omnipotent in the sense alluded to. I have alluded to it only for the sake of example, in order to refute the argument of omnipotence.

. . . .

HOW THE PROVINCES CAN BAFFLE FEDERAL USURPATION.

Mr. Blake continued :—

"I lay down this proposition with the utmost confidence: that each of those Provinces which come together and surrender up a portion of their independent powers, upon certain specific conditions, to the General Government, through the medium of the Imperial Legislature, have the right, and are bound in defence of the rights of the Province, to say to the supreme authority, if it is proposed to violate the compact: 'Step in and prevent that violation; protect us from the wrong proposed to be done; protect us from the injury which is proposed to be committed, not by a false course of policy, not by a misjudged use of the powers which we have given; but by an un-

---

*The legality of the action of the Federal Parliament in altering the terms of the B. N. A. Act, in the matter of the Nova Scotia Subsidy.

warrantable usurpation of authority in excess of those powers." (Hear, hear.)

THE PROVINCES CAN APPLY FOR AN AMENDMENT OF THE CONSTITUTION.

Mr. Blake proceeded:—

" I maintain, secondly that each Province has the right to apply to the same supreme authority to ask any needed amendment of the Constitution. Those who had authority to address Her Majesty to make this Constitution, would have authority to address Her Majesty to unmake or to destroy it."

CHAPTER XVII.

PREROGATIVE CLAIMS SET ASIDE—CONSTITUTIONAL VICTORY FOR ONTARIO AND QUEBEC.

THE Lieutenant-Governor of Ontario, on the 24th of March, 1874, assented to "An Act to amend the Law respecting Escheats and Forfeitures."

Colonel H. Bernard, Deputy Minister of Justice, made on the 18th of Nov., 1874, a Report against the statute. The Report is in part as follows:[*]

" The Act provides, in effect, that whenever lands, &c.,

---

[*] Sessional Papers, Can., 1877, No. 89, p. 88.

situate in Ontario have (1) escheated to the Crown by reason of intestacy without lawful heirs, or have (2) become forfeited, whether for treason or felony or any other cause, the Attorney-General may cause possession of such lands, &c., to be taken in the name of the Crown.

"It also provides that the Lieutenant-Governor in Council may grant lands which may be so escheated or become forfeited, with a view of restoration to any of the family of the person to whom they had belonged, and the same, without entry or inquest of office being found.

"The Act also provides that the Lieutenant-Governor in Council may make any assignment of personal property to which the Crown is entitled, (1) by reason of the person last entitled thereto having died intestate, without kin or other persons entitled to succeed thereto, or (2) by reason of forfeiture of the same to the Crown; and further, that the Lieutenant-Governor may waive or release the right of the Crown in such property.

"The undersigned is strongly inclined to entertain the opinion that this law is not within the competency of a Local Legislature, upon the following grounds, viz:

"First, as to Escheats.—

"The law of England (except in so far as the same may have been affected in England by Statute law, not applicable to Canada), prevails in the Province of Ontario.

"No prerogative rights of the Crown are vested in the Lieutenant-Governor of a Province, unless it be under the British North America Act; nor does his commission, issued by the Governor-General under the Great Seal of

Canada, confer on him the right of using or exercising any prerogative.

"There would, therefore, be no authority in the Lieutenant-Governor to exercise the prerogative of the Crown in respect to escheat, nor would the Legislature have competence to deal with such right or to confer any powers on the Lieutenant-Governor in respect thereof; nor would the Queen be bound by any acts of a Local Legislature in "respect to property and civil rights" arising in regard to her Crown. If, however, they lay claim under the 109th section of the British North America Act, 1867, the latter cannot apply, inasmuch as that section has reference alone to lands belonging to the Province of Canada . . . . at the date of the Union, and, in such case, the section would give no power to Ontario to deal with such lands as might become escheated to the Crown since the date of the Union, 1st July, 1867.

"Second, as to Forfeitures.—

"The forfeiture of lands or personal property for treason or felony (or for other cause than forfeiture for want of heirs) is also a matter of prerogative right of the Crown, the power of granting the same after the forfeiture has accrued to the Crown has not by the British North America Act been conferred upon a Province or its Lieutenant-Governor, and it must still therefore continue to be administered by the Governor-General of Canada as Her Majesty's representative.

"The Act of Ontario tends to confer power on the

Lieutenant-Governor in Council to restore lands or personal property forfeited for crime to the family of the person to whom the same had belonged. This is in effect giving the power to exercise an attribute of pardon, in the prerogative of mercy.

"Moreover, forfeiture is to be regarded as a matter of criminal law and criminal procedure—subjects which, by section 91 of the British North America Act, sub-section 27, are within the exclusive Legislative jurisdiction of the Parliament of Canada.

"In either view, therefore, whether as affecting Her Majesty's prerogative or as entrenching upon the criminal law or criminal procedure, the undersigned is of opinion that the Legislature of a Province has no power to legislate in respect to forfeitures to the Crown of land or personal property.

"The undersigned is equally of opinion that under the head of 'property and civil rights,' no Provincial Legislature can exercise authority in respect to the right of the Crown to the personal property of an intestate leaving no persons capable of inheriting.

"The undersigned recommends that communication should be had with the Lieutenant-Governor of Ontario to the above effect, suggesting that the Act in question is beyond the legislative competence of the Legislature of Ontario, and that the same should therefore be repealed."

Hon. Attorney-General Mowat, in one of the ablest State Papers, in both a legal and Constitutional aspect, that has appeared since Confederation, took up the challenge thrown down by the Deputy Minister of Justice, at Ottawa.

The reply of Hon. Mr. Mowat is dated Toronto, 17th of February, 1875. It is, in part, as follows :

REPLY OF HON. ATTORNEY-GENERAL MOWAT.

" The undersigned has had under consideration the Report of the Deputy Minister of Justice, dated 18th November, 1874, with reference to the Act to amend the law respecting Escheats and Forfeitures, passed 24th March, 1874, which Report was concurred in by the Minister of Justice and approved by an order of the Privy Council, dated 27th November.

" The undersigned ventures to affirm (notwithstanding the arguments of the Deputy Minister of Justice to the contrary) that the Act in question was not *ultra vires*, but was entirely within the authority of the Legislature to pass, and that, if this is not clear, the proper course will appear to be, confirmatory legislation on the part of the Dominion Parliament, and not the disallowance of the Act or its enforced repeal.

" 1. With regard to the right to such property, and to the jurisdiction to legislate respecting it : it is to be remembered that, while property of this kind in the British North America Provinces before Confederation was in the Queen's name, as all other public property was, and is, it did not belong to Her Majesty personally, and for her private use ; nor did it belong to the empire at large. On the contrary, such property, like ungranted and unappropriated wild lands, belonged to the provinces. And the provinces have still all former rights which have not been taken from them, or which they have not themselves parted with.

"The Confederation Act contains no clause repealing the old constitutional Acts which governed the provinces, or declaring that all unenumerated rights founded upon, or derived under the former Acts, or otherwise possessed by the Provinces, were to lease, or were to vest in the Dominion; and it is not pretended that the Act contains any provision which would give this property in the Dominion, if a provision for that purpose is necessary.

"Either, therefore, escheated and forfeited property belongs still to the Provinces, or the Crown at Confederation resumed all provincial rights which the Confederation Act did not deal with, an alternative which is wholly unsupportable, and which the undersigned trusts that the authorities of the Dominion, as well as those of all the Provinces, will at all times unite in repudiating. The undersigned assumes it to be undeniable, that all rights of the Provinces as they existed before Confederation have, by the Confederation Act, been divided between the Dominion and the Provinces, and that whatever has not been given to the former is retained by the latter.

"The undersigned submits that these considerations (not touched upon by the report of the Deputy Minister of Justice) are absolutely conclusive on the present question, for if escheated and forfeited property belongs to the Provinces, the Provincial Legislatures have certainly a right to deal with it as falling under the head of 'Property and civil rights in the Province;'

"2. But the express language of the British North America Act happens to contain enough to establish the same view affirmatively from the Act itself. Lands, mines, minerals, royalties and other "public property," (an expression which in English law includes personal property as well as real) theretofore belonging to each Province, are, by the 109th and 117th sections, declared to continue to belong to such Province, still, however, being and continuing to be in Her Majesty's name, but having long before, by express recognizance or tacit agreement, become to all intents and purposes the property of the Provinces to be used and administered by the Provincial authorities, for the use and advantages of the Provinces; so that such property, in the view of the Imperial Parliament, "belonged" to the Provinces before the passing of the British North America Act. Such was the right of the Provinces, not only with regard to lands which had never been the subject of grant by the Crown, but to lands also which had been sold by the Crown, but not patented; and to lands which had once been granted, but had subsequently been surrendered for Provincial use, and to lands in respect to which Her Majesty had any sort of right or interest in trust for the Provinces. The lands and other public property thus undoubtedly belonging to the Provinces amount to many thousand times more in extent and value than all the escheated and forfeited property which will come into existence in half a century.

"Now escheat is one of the few remaining incidents of the feudal tenure, and arose under the old feudal system *per defectum sanguinis,* from the want of a tenant to perform the services to the lord of whom the land was held, or *per defectum tenentis,* by corruption of blood by attainder. The escheat was not to the Crown unless the Crown happened to be also the lord of whom the land was held; and many of the lands in England were held of mesne lords, and not of the Crown.

"This right of escheat was called by the old writers a species of reversion.

"All the lands in Ontario are held of the Crown, and not of a mesne lord, and the Crown retains in them (though limited by modern legislation) this right of escheat.

"On ordinary principles of construction the right so retained must be taken to have been included, and was included, like a reversion after a grant heretofore made for life or years, in the general words of the 109th and 117th sections of the British North America Act. It is impossible to suppose, (and nobody does, in fact, suppose,) that the Imperial Parliament meant to except such a right from the operation of these sections, and what Parliament must be taken to have meant, is the test of what any enactment legally signifies.

"The doctrine of the report would deprive all the Maritime Provinces of *maritima incrementa,* and of lands become *derelict* by the sudden desertion of the sea. These belong to the Queen by her prerogative, but, under our system of Confederation, the trust would surely be for the Provinces, and not for the Dominion ; and if the trust is for the Provinces, the Provinces have a right to legislate and deal with such lands to the same extent, and in the same way, as they deal with other Crown lands which belong to the Provinces.

" The Deputy Minister of Justice thinks that the circumstances of the right to escheats and forfeitures being a prerogative right, affords an argument against the Ontario Act.

" The undersigned disputes this notion. The recognized modern doctrine is, that all prerogative rights are trusts for the benefit of the people ; and it is easy to demonstrate that, far more of what is prerogative falls within the acknowledged authority of the Provinces than within the authority assigned to the Dominion, and that many prerogative duties and rights devolve upon the Lieutenant-Governor, not by the express terms of ' The British North America Act,' but from the nature of the office which he holds. Thus, grants from Provincial Governments continue of necessity to be made in the Queen's name ; and all proceedings in the Provinces for the administration of Justice, which, before Confederation, were in the Queen's name, continue of necessity to be in the Queen's name still.

" In practice the Provincial Statutes also are expressed to be by Her Majesty, with the advice and consent of the Legislative Assembly ; and the Lieutenant-Governor, before proroguing Parliament, assents, in the Queen's name, to the Bills which have been passed. If one thing more than another is matter of prerogative, it is the administration of justice. The Sovereign is said, by legal and Constitutional writers, to be the 'fountain of justice,' and to have an 'inherent right' inseparable from the Crown, to distribute 'justice' amongst His or Her subjects. So it is said to be the Sovereign prerogative 'to see to the execution of the laws;' and by the 9th Section of the Confederation Act 'the Executive Government and authority of and over Canada is declared to continue and be vested in the Queen.' This plainly includes the Executive Government and authority of the Province as well as of the Dominion; the executive authority under the Act being executed partly by the Governor-General, and partly by the Lieutenant-Governors. When the British North America Act commences to set out the provisional constitutions, the first subject treated of is under the head of 'Executive Power,' The Lieutenant-Governor, or any one discharging the duty of the Lieutenant-Governor, is called in the 62nd Section 'the Chief Executive Officer.' The 63rd Section provides for an 'Executive Council' in Ontario and Quebec. The 64th Section declares that 'the constitution of the Executive authority in Nova Scotia and New Brunswick shall, subject to the provisions of the Act, continue as it existed at the Union, until altered under the authority of the Act.' The 65th Section provides that, all powers, authorities and functions which, under any Imperial or Provincial Act were, at the Union, 'vested in, or exerciseable by the respective Governors or Lieutenant Governors' shall, as far as the same are capable of being exercised after the Union, in relation to the Governments of Ontario and Quebec, respectively, be vested in and exercised by the Lieutenant-Governors under the new system. And by the 82nd Section it is directed that the Lieutenant-Governors of Ontario and Quebec shall, 'from time to time, in the Queen's name, . . summon and call together the Legislative Assembly of the Province.' The Act gives no full enumeration or general statement of the duties of the Lieutenant-Governor. To a large extent his duties and authorities are left to be implied and inferred from his character as as Lieutenant-Governor or 'Chief Executive Officer,' and from the known Constitutional rights and duties theretofore belonging to the office of a Lieutenant-Governor, so far as relates to the Government and Legislation of the Provinces.

"So, also another prerogative of the Sovereign, according to English law, is the care of the persons and property of minors, lunatics and idiots. It has not hitherto been doubted, (and the undersigned apprehends there is no reason for doubting), that Provincial Legislatures have their property under their control; and since Confederation various Provincial Acts have from time to time been passed with respect to them, which the Dominion authorities never questioned on this ground, and which our Courts have recognized and acted upon as valued laws. There is nothing in the 'British North America Act' devolving this prerogative upon the Governor or Legislature of the Province, unless it is to be found in some of those general provisions which the undersigned has already quoted.

" These considerations show that there is no reason for presuming against a claim of the Provinces, though the subject may be what is technically, matter of prerogative, and has not been expressly assigned to the Lieutenant-Governors.

" The undersigned may add that on coming into office he found that the Governments of the late Mr. Sandfield Macdonald and Mr. Blake had regarded escheated and forfeited property as belonging to the Province, and as within provincial jurisdiction, and had acted on that view.

" The Surrogate Court here, and the Court of Chancery also, have assumed the jurisdiction to be provincial, and acted accordingly.

"It thus appears that the jurisdiction of a Provincial Legislature and Executive to deal with such matters rests on the strongest grounds, and that none of the objections suggested to the Act are sustainable ; and the undersigned has considerable confidence that the Minister of Justice and his Deputy will on consideration coincide in this conclusion.

" (Signed)   O. MOWAT.

"*17th February, 1875.*"

Hon. M. Fournier, Minister of Justice, under date of March 26, 1875, replied to Hon. Attorney-General Mowat. He concludes as follows :—

"Upon a reconsideration of the case, the undersigned is unable to arrive at any other conclusion than the following:—

"*Firstly,*—That escheat is a matter of prerogative which is not by the British North America Act, 1867, vested in a Provincial Government or Legislature.

"*Secondly,*—That it is not one of the subjects coming within the enumeration of subjects left exclusively to Provincial Legislatures.

"*Thirdly,*—That a Provincial Legislature, by its very statutable composition, has no power to deal with prerogatives of the Crown.

"*Fourthly,*—That the Lieutenant-Governor has not under the Statute, or by his commission, any power to deal with prerogatives of the Crown; and not being empowered to assent in the Queen's name to any law of a Provincial Legislature, he cannot bind Her Majesty's prerogative rights.

"*Fifthly,*—That the 109th and 117th sections of the British North America Act, 1867, refer only to lands and public property of the several Provinces at the date of the union, subject to the reservations in Section 108, and schedule 3.

"*Sixthly,*—That escheat cannot be dealt with under Section 92, sub-section 5, in respect to the management and sale of the public lands belonging to the Province; or sub-section 13, as to property and civil rights in the Province; or sub-section 16, as being a matter of a merely local or private nature in the Province.

"*Seventhly*,—That forfeiture for want of heirs is virtually escheat, and that forfeiture for crime and corruption of blood, is a matter of criminal procedure.

"He, therefore, feels it incumbent to advise that the Act of the Legislature of the Province of Ontario, passed on the 24th day of March, 1874, entitled:

"An Act to amend the Law respecting Escheats and Forfeitures" be disallowed by Your Excellency in Council.

"(Signed)   T. FOURNIER,
"*Minister of Justice.*"

The Earl of Dufferin, by an Order in Council, dated 1st April 1875, declared his disallowance of the Act.

But the matter was not yet decided.

Hon. Edward Blake, Minister of Justice, under date of Ottawa, 18th of October 1876, drew up a memorandum which, on the 25th of October, was approved by the Governor-General in Council.

The memorandum was in part as follows:—

"The undersigned begs to refer to the Order in Council of 19th May, 1876, upon the subject of escheats and forfeitures, and to the various reports upon the same subject. In the report on which that Order was founded, the undersigned recommended a reference to the Supreme Court, with the consent of the Province of Ontario, of certain questions, with a view of disposing of the legal point involved.

"The undersigned was led to recommend this course, for the following reasons:

"1st. With reference to forfeitures for treason, or other like cause, it was, as it is, the opinion of the undersigned, that such forfeitures appertain exclusively to Canada.

"2nd. With reference to escheats and forfeitures of land and personal property for want of heirs and representatives, although the opinion of the undersigned was adverse to the pretensions of Canada, yet the views entertained by his predecessors on this subject, and the course of action which had been pursued by the Government, seemed to him to render it improper that he should recommend the abandonment of the position, theretofore, taken without a solemn, judicial decision. The undersigned was not insensible of some inconvenience which might arise from the presentation of the question in the manner proposed, but it seemed, at that time, to be, upon the whole, the best mode of reaching a solution. Since that time, however, a judgment, which had been obtained in the Superior Court of Quebec, in favour of the rights of Canada, has been appealed, and by the unanimous judgment of the Court of Queen's Bench, Appeal side, of Quebec, composed of Mr. Chief-Justice Dorion, Mr. Justice Monck, Mr. Justice Ramsay, Mr. Justice Sanborn and Mr. Justice Tessier, reversed.

"The undersigned refers to a copy of this judgment, which he appends to this report. It appears to the undersigned that the more correct mode of obtaining the decision of the Supreme Court would be by prosecuting an appeal from that judgment; but independent of a question which arises as to the practicability of appealing, the undersigned is disposed to attach much weight to the unanimous judgment to which he has referred, and he is of opinion that it has so altered the circumstances as to render proper the adoption of a different course by the Government of Canada.

"The undersigned has reason to believe that the Government of Ontario is prepared to assent to the plan which he is about to propose. The undersigned recommends that the Order in Council of 19th May be rescinded, and—

"1. That for the future, unless there should be a judicial decision overruling that to which he has referred, the Government should act upon the assumption that lands and personal property in any Province escheated or forfeited by reason of intestacy without lawful heirs or next of kin, or other persons entitled to succeed, are subjects appertaining to the Province, and within its legislative competence, and that the Government of Canada should decline to interfere in such matters.

"2. That for the future, as in the past, unless there should be a judicial decision establishing the contrary view, the Government of Canada should act upon the assumption that lands and personal property forfeited to the Crown for treason, felony or other like cause, are subjects appertaining to Canada, and within its legislative competence.

"3. That in pursuance of this policy, the Government should leave to their operation Provincial statutes otherwise unobjectionable, dealing with the first of these subjects, but should disallow Provincial statutes dealing with the second of them.

"(Signed) EDWARD BLAKE."

The following is the Quebec case to which Hon. Mr. Blake refers:—

In the Court of Appeal, Qeubec, September 8th, 1876, there were present, the Honourables A. A. Dorion, Chief Justice; Mr. Justice Monk, Mr. Justice Ramsay, Mr. Justice Sanborn, Mr. Justice Tessier.

The Attorney-General for the Province of Quebec (Plaintiff in the Court below), Appellant, and Damase Caron, of the Parish of St. Patrice de la Rivière du Loup, Burgess (Defendant in the Court below), and the Attorney-General for the Dominion of Canada (Intervening party in the Court below), Respondent.

"The Court considering that the late Edward Fraser, whose estate is claimed by the Hon. Attorney-General for the Province of Quebec, acting also in this behalf for Her Majesty, the Queen, died at Rivière du Loup, in the Province of Quebec, about the second day of February, 1874, without heirs and intestate, and according to the pretensions of both parties, he left an estate which hath escheated to the Crown. And considering this is one of the sources of revenue which, as a minor prerogative of the Crown, was yielded up to the respective Provinces now confederated into the Dominion of Canada, prior to the Union of the Provinces of Canada, Nova Scotia and

New Brunswick, and that such escheat prior to the said Union formed part of the revenues of respective Provinces where they arose.

" And considering that by the British North America Act of 1867, such revenues as were subject to the appropriation of the respective Legislatures of Canada, Nova Scotia and New Brunswick, and which are revised by the several Provinces since the Union, in accordance with the special powers ·conferred upon them by that Act, belong to said Provinces. And considering as having jurisdiction over the law of descents by virtue of its jurisdiction over property and civil rights in the Province under said Act, the Legislature of the Province of Quebec is invested with power to appropriate this casual revenue to itself.

"And considering that amongst other things, it is declared by the said British North America Act of 1867, that all royalties belonging to the several Provinces of Canada, Nova Scotia and New Brunswick, at the Union, shall belong to the several Provinces of Ontario, Quebec, Nova Scotia and New Brunswick, in which the same are situated or arise, and that escheats such as the one in question, are royalties.

" And considering that such estate is composed of real as well as personal property, and that all territorial Crown rights and privileges possessed by the late Provinces of Canada, Nova Scotia, and New Brunswick, before the union thereof into the Dominion of Canada, have been at the Union given to the several Provinces of Ontario, Quebec, Nova Scotia and New Brunswick, and the law of escheats by reason of want of heirs, is of feudal origin, and cognate with the law of tenures.

"And considering that by the general tenor of the Act of union and the division of assets and revenues, it is manifest that a casual local revenue, like the one in question, was intended to be left to the local Province.

"And, therefore, considering that there is error in the judgment rendered in this cause in the Superior Court at Kamouraska, in the 29th day of January, 1876, and now in appeal in maintaining the intervention of the Hon. the Attorney-General for the Dominion of Canada claiming said estate of the said late Edward Fraser as belonging to the Dominion of Canada, and not the Province of Quebec, doth reverse the said judgment, and proceeding to render the judgment which the Court below ought to have rendered, doth maintain the appeal of the Attorney-General for the Province of Quebec in this cause, and doth reject the petition in intervention of said Attorney-General for the Dominion of Canada.

"And it is further ordered that the record be remitted to the Superior Court at Kamouraska.

"A true copy.

" (Signed)   F. LANGELIER."

The Lieut.-Governor of Ontario, in Council, 24th of November, 1876, approved of a Report of Attorney-General Mowat, in respect to the Order of the Governor-General, in Council, 25th October, 1876.

The Reports quote the recommendations 1 and 2 made

by the Minister of Justice in his Memorandum of the 18th of October, and concludes as follows :—

"The undersigned has already, in former reports, fully treated of the matters in dispute between this Government and the Dominion with reference to this subject, and he is of opinion that the plan of action adopted by the said Order, as, upon the whole, a fair settlement of the matters in dispute, and he, therefore, recommends that, until a judicial decision be given establishing the contrary to be the law, this Government acts upon the assumptions adopted by the said Order in Council for the guidance of the Dominion Government hereinbefore fully set out.

"(Signed)   O. MOWAT."

CHAPTER XVIII.

THE PROVINCIAL APPOINTMENT OF QUEEN'S COUNSEL.

THE opinion has been hazarded that the Lieut.-Governors of the Provinces have not the power to confer the title of Queen's Counsel. It has been maintained, on the other hand, that they do possess this prerogative. The question, in one aspect, is of interest to the Bar; in another, it is of importance to the public, because it involves a right intimately bound up with the prerogatives the Provinces possess in the matter of "the administration of justice."*

---

* See Section 92 of the B. N. A. Act, Sub-section 14.

On the 3rd of January, 1872, Sir John A. Macdonald made a Report to the Governor-General, which is, in part as follows :—

" The undersigned has the honour to report to Your Excellency, that the question has been raised by the Government of the Province of Nova Scotia as to whether they have the power of appointing Queen's Counsel for the Province, their opinion being that they have no such power.

" The undersigned is of opinion that, as a matter of course, Her Majesty has directly, as well as through her representative the Governor-General, the power of selecting from the Bars of the several Provinces, her own counsel, and, as *fons honoris*, of giving them such precedence and pre-audience in her Courts as she thinks proper.

" It is held by some that the Lieutenant-Governors of the Provinces, as they are now not appointed directly by Her Majesty, but by the Governor-General, under the British North America Act, 1867, clause 58, do not represent her sufficiently to exercise the Royal prerogative, without positive statutory enactment.

" This seems to have been the view of Her Majesty's Government in 1864, when they refused to confer the pardoning powers on the Lieutenant-Governors. (See despatch of Mr. Cardwell of 3rd December, 1864 ; also Lord Granville's despatch of 24th February, 1869.) On the other hand, it is contended that the 64th and 65th clauses continue to the Lieutenant-Governors the powers of appointing Queen's Counsel which they exercised while holding Commissions under the Great Seal of England.

"Reference is also made to the 63rd Section by which the Lieutenant-Governors of Ontario and Quebec appoint Attorney - Generals, and the Lieutenant - Governor of Quebec also a Solicitor-General.

"It will be seen that by the 92nd clause of the Act, it is provided that 'the Legislature of each Province may make laws in relation to the Administration of Justice in the Province, including the constitution, maintenance and organization of Provincial Courts, both of civil and criminal jurisdiction, and, including procedure in civil matters in those Courts.'

"Under this power, the undersigned is of opinion that the Legislature of a Province, being charged with the administration of justice and the organization of the Courts, may, by Statute, provide for the general conduct of business before those Courts; and may make such provisions with respect to the Bar, the management of criminal prosecutions by counsel, the selection of those counsel, and the right of pre-audience, as it sees fit. Such enactment must, however, in the opinion of the undersigned, be subject to the exercise of the Royal prerogative, which is paramount, and in no way diminished by the terms of the Act of Confederation. As the matter affects Her Majesty's prorogative, the undersigned would respectfully recommend that it be submitted to the Right Honourable the Secretary of State for the Colonies, for the opinion of the Law Officers of the Crown, and for Her Majesty's decision thereon.

"The questions for opinion would seem to be :—

"(1.) Has the Governor-General (since 1st July, 1867, when the Union came into effect), power, as Her Majesty's representative, to appoint Queen's Counsel ?

"(2.) Has a Lieutenant-Governor, appointed since that date, the power of appointment ?

"(3.) Can the Legislature of a Province confer by Statute on its Lieutenant-Governor the power of appointing Queen's Counsel ?

"(4.) If these questions are answered in the affirmative, how is the question of precedence or pre-audience to be settled ?

"All which is respectively submitted.

"(Signed)   JOHN A. MACDONALD."

The Earl of Kimberley's answer to the four questions propounded by Sir John A. Macdonald "for the opinion of the Law Officers of the Crown, and for Her Majesty's decision thereon," must be regarded as conclusive. It was as follows :—

"*The Earl of Kimberley to Lord Lisgar.*

"DOWNING STREET, *1st February, 1872.*

"MY LORD,—In compliance with the request contained in your despatch, No. 1 of the 4th January, I have taken the opinion of the Law Officers of the Crown on the questions raised therein, with regard to the power of appointing Queen's Counsel in the Provinces forming the Dominion. I am advised that the Governor-General has now power, as Her Majesty's representative, to appoint Queen's Counsel, but that a Lieutenant-Governor appointed since the Union came into effect, has no such power of appointment.

"I am further advised that the Legislature of a Province can confer by Statute on its Lieutenant-Governor the power of appointing Queen's Counsel; and, with respect to precedence or pre-audience in the Courts of the Province, the Legislature of the Province has power to decide as between Queen's Counsel appointed by the Governor-General and the Lieutenant-Governor, as above explained.

"I have, &c.,
"(Signed)   KIMBERLEY.

"*Governor-General the Right Hon. Lord Lisgar, &c.*"

On the 28th of September, 1872, a memorandum was drawn up by Sir John A. Macdonald, respecting certain appointments to the honour of Queen's Counsel, which were made by the Lieutenant-Governor of Ontario, and gazetted on the 16th of March of that year.

The Minister of Justice, after referring to the despatch of the Earl of Kimberley, of 1st February, 1872, goes on to say:

"That, under the circumstances, great doubt must exist as to the validity of the commissions issued to the gentlemen named. . . . . . That, as the gentlemen mentioned are fully qualified to perform the duties of Her Majesty's counsel, the Minister of Justice recommends that commissions be issued by the Government of Canada to those gentlemen, or such of them as desire to receive the same."

This memorandum was followed by a communication from the Department of the Secretary of State to some of the gentlemen, who, on the 16th of March, had been, by the Lieutenant-Governor of Ontario, appointed Queen's counsel.

The communication was as follows:

"OTTAWA, *7th October, 1872.*

" SIR,—I have the honour to inform you that, the question having been raised in the Province of Nova Scotia as to where the power of appointing Queen's Counsel rested since the union of the Provinces, His Excellency the Governor-General, on the 4th January last, obtained, through the Right Honourable the Secretary of State for the Colonies, the opinion of the Law Officers of the Crown in England on the subject. These officers advised that the Governor-General has now the power, as Her Majesty's Representative, to appoint Queen's Counsel, but that a Lieutenant-Governor appointed since the Union came into effect, has, in the absence of legislation, no such power of appointment.

" Under these circumstances, and to remove all possible doubt as to the legality of your status as one of Her Majesty's Counsel for the Province of Ontario, I am commanded by His Excellency the Governor-General to inform you that a commission will be issued under the Great Seal of Canada, appointing you Queen's Counsel for Ontario, should you desire it.

"E. PARENT,
"*Under-Secretary of State.*"

Hon. Edward Blake was First Minister of the Province of Ontario when the appointments to which exception was taken, had been made. The opinion of his Government, on the issues involved in this letter from the Department of State, was embodied in the following copy of a Minute of Council, approved by His Excellency the Lieutenant-Governor, on the 23rd of October, 1872:

"The Committee of Council regret that the Government of Canada, entertaining the view that the opinion of the Law Officers referred to in this letter was applicable to Ontario, should not have thought fit to transmit a copy of it for Your Excellency's information. Although Your Excellency's Government is of opinion that Your Excellency is invested with the power to make such appointments without legislation, yet had they been made aware of the view of the Law Officers, they would have thought it proper to propose the legislation requisite for the removal of any possible doubt on the subject; and, having now become aware of it, it is their intention to propose such legislation during the Session which is to commence within a few weeks. It appears to the Committee that grave inconveniences and complications may arise from the proposed action of the Government of Canada.

"The Committee entertain the view that appointments of this description fall properly within the Local and not within the Federal jurisdiction, and they trust that, having regard to their expressed intentions as to legislation, the Government of Canada may see fit to abstain at present from issuing the proposed commissions.

"Should that Government, however, be of opinion that, notwithstanding the proposed legislation, the power of issuing such commission would remain with and should be exercised by His Excellency the Governor-General, it appears to the Committee that, before acting on that view, the opinion of the Judicial Committee of the Privy Council should be taken on a joint case to be argued on behalf of the respective Governments.

"The Committee purposely abstain from entering into any discussion of the Constitutional point; but they are bound to state that, in their opinion, the proposed action involves questions of Local and Federal jurisdiction far wider than the single question under discussion, and this renders them more anxious that the course they propose should commend itself to His Excellency the Governor-General."

"J. G. SCOTT,
"*Clerk, Executive Council.*

"*25th October, 1872.*"

The following is, in part, a copy of a Report of the Committee of the Privy Council on the foregoing minute of the Executive Council of Ontario, which Report was approved by the Governor-General, Dec. 13, 1872 :

" The Committee beg leave to report :

" That no appointments of Queen's Counsel for Ontario have yet been made by the Governor-General.

" The Executive Council of Ontario recommend a reference of this question to the Judicial Committee of the Privy Council.

" Had this suggestion been made before the assumption of the power of appointment by the Provincial Government, it might properly have been adopted, but under present circumstances it would seem that the question should be dealt with in the first instance, by the courts in Ontario.

" The Committee of Council do not apprehend that any inconveniences or complications can arise from the Queen's representative exercising the Royal prerogative in making such appointments.

" It is obvious that when the Supreme Court or other Dominion Courts are established, commissions issued by the Lieutenant-Governor would not, as of right, give precedence or position in those Courts. At the same time it might be advisable that such commissions should be recognized.

" The Committee of Council are, therefore, on the whole, of opinion that His Excellency the Governor-General, as the Queen's representative, should not refrain from appointing Her Majesty's Counsel; but they think an arrangement might advantageously be made between the Government of the Dominion and the several Provinces, by which Queen's Counsel, appointed by the Governor-General, would receive proper status and position in the Provincial Courts, and commissions issued under statutory authority by the Lieutenant-Governor would be recognized in the Courts of the Dominion.

The Government of Ontario was prompt to carry into effect the powers vested in the Legislature of the Province.

The Lieutenant-Governor of Ontario, on the 29th of March, 1873, assented to the two following Statutes :—

" An Act respecting the Appointing of Queen's Counsel." (36 Vic., cap. 3.)

" An Act to regulate the proceedings of the Bar of Ontario." (36 Vic., cap. 4.)

The preamble to the first-mentioned of these statutes explains clearly and forcibly the reasons which justify its enactment. They are as follow :—

" Whereas in the course of the administration of justice, matters between the Crown and the subject are brought, some in Her Majesty's name and some in the name of the Attorney-General for Ontario, before Her Majesty's Courts in Ontario by the direction and under the control and management of the Provincial Government ; And whereas the Lieutenant-Governor of right ought to have the power to appoint, from among the members of the Bar of Ontario, Provincial officers who may assist in the conduct of such matters on behalf of the Crown, under the name of Her Majesty's Counsel learned in the law of the said Province ; And whereas doubts have been cast on the power of the Lieutenant-Governor to make such appointments, and it is expedient to remove such doubts: Therefore, &c."

The authority to pass these Statutes is two-fold—

1. It is conferred by the 92nd Section of the B. N. A. Act, sub-Section 14; which places under Provincial control—

"The Administration of Justice in the Province, including the constitution, maintenance, and organization of Provincial Courts, both of civil and criminal jurisdiction, and including procedure in civil matters in those Courts."

2. It is conferred after the manner suggested in the 2nd paragraph of the Earl of Kimberley's despatch to Lord Lisgar, 1st February, 1872.

The Law Officers of the Crown must be considered to have formed their opinion without prejudice or predisposition. That opinion was a virtual judgment on issues submitted by the Canadian Government. That judgment the Imperial Government accepted, and, acting on it, gave to the Provincial Legislatures the authority to invest the Lieutenant-Governors with power to appoint Queen's Counsel. This authority, since that time they have possessed. Further, they must continue to possess it, until a Colonial Tribunal is authorized to overrule the judgment of those eminent Jurists on whose opinions the Imperial Government is wont to base its action, in dealing with Constitutional issues that arise from time to time in the dependencies of the British Empire.

CHAPTER XIX.

WHO ARE THE PRESENT QUEEN'S COUNSEL IN ONTARIO?

THE official correspondence relating to the Provincial prerogatives, in the matter of the appointment of Queen's Counsel is now before the reader. Upon this correspondence, any one understanding the English language, can form a judgment which shall be as sound and sensible as that of any lawyer. In this particular case there would seem to be little or no room for the display of those eccentric mental performances which are veiled under the euphemism of "a conflict of legal opinions."

In defence of the power of the Provincial Legislatures to invest the Lieutenant-Governors with the prerogative to appoint Queen's Counsel, there is a phalanx of legal authority impossible to be broken. In that phalanx stand Sir John A. Macdonald, the Law Officers of the Crown in England, Hon. Edward Blake. Next, in order of time, comes Hon. Oliver Mowat, Attorney-General and first Minister of the Province of Ontario, a public man, accustomed, in a long official career, to deal with the exigencies of practical statesmanship, and a jurist in whom conscientiousness, caution and legal learning are alike conspicuous.

Then there are the seven gentlemen, who were gazetted on the 16th of March, 1872, as having been appointed

Queen's Counsel by the Lieutenant-Governor of Ontario. Six of these eminent lawyers have since ascended the Bench. Their names are as follows:—

Chief Justice Moss, Chief Justice Wood, Justice Patterson, Justice Anderson, Vice-Chancellor Blake, Vice-Chancellor Proudfoot.

It is only right to mention the names of a few of the learned gentlemen who, at the present moment in this Province, wear the title of Queen's Counsel. On the Conservative side, are Hon. Alexander Morris, a gentleman of large and varied experience in public life, who has been a Cabinet Minister, the Chief Justice of a Province, and its Lieutenant-Governor. Then there is Mr. William Ralph Meredith, whose reputation as a lawyer is well earned, and whose abilities have won for him the leadership of the Ontario Opposition in the Provincial Parliament. Again, there is Mr. W. H. Scott, the member for West Peterborough, a lawyer of high standing in his profession; along with him, Mr. Dalton McCarthy.

On the Liberal side of politics are to be found wearing the honour of Queen's Counsel by right of their own ability, as well as Provincial authority, such men as Hon. T. B. Pardee, Hon. C. F. Fraser, Hon. A. S. Hardy, and Mr. J. G. Scott, Deputy Attorney-General.

The inquiry now arises: Are all the authorities who have pronounced on this question, beginning with the Law Officers of the Crown, likely to be wrong, and the Supreme Court likely to be right? The question answers itself in an energetic negative.

CHAPTER XX.

CAN THE GOVERNOR-GENERAL APPOINT QUEEN'S COUNSEL?

THE Governor-General of Canada performs the duties of his office in accordance with a series of regulations which are known as the "Royal Instructions." Amongst other appointments which, since the Union year, 1841, the Governors-General have been accustomed to make, are those of Queen's Counsel.

The question now arises, by what authority did the Governors-General of the late Province of Canada appoint Queen's Counsel? If their authority is not contained in the Royal Instructions, whence is it derived?* In the Royal Instructions to Lord Sydenham,† no such authority is conferred. The Royal Instructions to Sir Edmund W. Head ‡ are silent on the subject. There is no reference to the matter in the Royal Instructions to Lord Monck. §

There is a vital and fundamental difference between the inherent prerogative of the Sovereign, and the delegated

---

* The earliest appointments after the Union were : Upper Canada, 1842 : Messrs. W. H. Draper, H. J. Boulton, R. Baldwin, H. Sherwood (precedence), J. E. Small. Lower Canada, 1842: Messrs. F. W. Primrose, C. S. Chervier, D. Fisher, C. R. Ogden, L. H. Lafontaine, T. C. Aylwin, A. N. Morin.

† Dated Downing Street, 7th December, 1839.

‡ Dated Balmoral, 20th September, 1854.

§ Dated Windsor, 2nd November, 1861.

prerogative. The Royal prerogative, although in its exercise sometimes to be questioned, is, nevertheless, an incident of Sovereign power, the origin of which is hidden away in the mists of our earliest political history. But the prerogative of a Governor-General is a power both recent and delegated. The Royal Instructions, which define and circumscribe the Vice-Regal prerogative, are submitted to Parliament and printed in the records.* They are thus open to investigation. They might, perhaps, on a motion of the House, be subject to alteration or revision by the Imperial authorities.

In none of the Royal Commissions, as we have shown, is there any express authority given to a Governor-General to appoint Queen's Counsel. In the Commission to the Marquis of Lorne, the only portion which can be tortured into an authorization to appoint Queen's Counsel, is the following paragraph:—

"And, We do further authorize and empower our said Governor-General to constitute and appoint, in Our name and on Our behalf, all such Judges, Commissioners, Justices of the Peace, and other necessary officers and Ministers of Our said Dominion, as may be lawfully constituted or appointed by Us."

It has been held by those who contend that the Governor-General has the sole right to make these appointments, that the words "other necessary officers" comprise in their

---

* See the Earl of Dufferin's Commission and Instructions, Journals of Canadian Commons, 1873, p. 85. See also Marquis of Lorne's Commission and Instructions, S. P. C., 1879, No. 14, p. 1.

meaning Queen's Counsel. But Mr. Justice Gwynne says:*—"For Queen's Counsel have never been, nor can they be, regarded as a necessary element in the constitution and organization of Courts, either of civil or criminal jurisdiction. . . . They are not in any sense Officers of the Courts, nor Provincial Officers."

On the other hand, the Consolidated Statutes of Upper Canada, Cap. 11, Sec. 3, declare :—

"The said Courts (Assize and Nisi Prius, etc.), shall be presided over by one of the Chief Justices, or of the Judges of the said Superior Courts, or in their absence, then by some one Judge of a County Court, or by some one of Her Majesty's Counsel learned in the Law of the Upper Canada Bar, upon such Judge or Counsel being requested by any one of the said Chief Justices or Judges of such Superior Courts to attend for that purpose."

Here is a conflict between statutory enactment and a judicial opinion. It would seem probable, however, that Mr. Justice Gwynne is correct. Queen's Counsel are not Officers of the Court in the proper sense of the word; for the incidents of permanence and continuance are bound up with the conception of officership. A Queen's Counsel, called upon suddenly to perform the functions of a Judge, is only an officer of the Court for the time being. The moment he leaves the Bench, the attributes of an Officer of the Court disappear along with him.

If a Queen's Counsel is no Officer of the Court, he cannot come under the designation "other necessary officers"

---

* Canada Law Journal, Dec., 1879, p. 316.

in the Royal Commission. The Governor-General, therefore, has no power to nominate to this honour.

There would seem to be no doubt, however, that the Federal Parliament can confer on the Governor-General the power to appoint Queen's Counsel, but for the Federal Courts only; just as the Local Legislatures, acting upon the opinion of the Law Officers of the Crown in England, conferred on the Lieutenant-Governors the power to appoint Queen's Counsel for the Provincial Courts. It may be considered that the opinion here expressed, calling in question the power of the Governor-General to appoint Queen's Counsel, tends to a limitation of the prerogative. But it is to be borne in mind, that, for a long series of years, the Law Officers of the Crown in England have recognized the right of the Imperial, as well as of the Colonial Legislatures, to affect, influence and modify, the prerogative in respect to its exercise in the Colonies.

In respect to the powers of the Crown to alter the Tenure of Lands in Canada, the Joint Opinion of the Attorney-General, Sir W. Garrow, and the Solicitor-General, Sir S. Shepherd, was given on the 22nd of January, 1817.* They say:—"We beg leave to observe that if it was intended to change the tenure of any lands without the consent or desire of the persons possessing such lands, or at once to affect a general alteration of tenure, there is no doubt that it could not be done without an Act of the Legislative bodies with the assent of His Majesty. . . There is, by the 43rd Section of 31 George III., Cap. 31, a

---

* Forsyth's Constitutional Law, pp. 153-154.

restriction of the prerogative as to the tenure on which lands shall be granted in Upper Canada, because by that Section His Majesty can only grant lands on free and common soccage."

Attorney-General Sir James Scarlett and Solicitor-General Sir N. C. Tindal gave, in 1827, a joint opinion on the power of the Crown to create the office of Master of the Rolls in Canada.* They say :

" We have duly considered the several matters referred to us, and have now the honour to report, for His Majesty's information, that the result of our investigation leaves us in considerable doubt whether His Majesty lawfully can, by letters patent under the Great Seal, or in any other manner, without the intervention of Parliament, or of the Local Legislature, create any new Judge in Equity, by whatsoever name he may be called, in Upper Canada. . . . . . It would be more expedient, if consistent with His Majesty's pleasure, that the intended Equity Judge should be called Vice-Chancellor to the Governor. . . . . . But in order to prevent doubts on the subject, we would recommend this to be done by the aid of Parliament or of the Local Legislature."

It will be seen, from the illustrations just given, that, in so far as respects Canada, two important prerogatives, the power of the Crown in matters of Tenure, and the establishment of a Court of Justice, could not be exercised without the consent of the Local Legislature.

It has been already stated that the Royal Commission

---

* Forsyth, pp. 172-174.

contains no explicit authority to appoint Queen's Counsel. It is not the first time that the Royal Commission and Instructions have been found inoperative or defective. So far back as 1738, Attorney-General Sir D. Ryder, and Solicitor-General Sir T. Strange, delivered a Joint Opinion on the erection of a Court of Exchequer in South Carolina.*

The Law Officers, replying to the question whether the Governor, by his Commission or Instructions, be sufficiently empowered to appoint a Chief Baron, said: "As doubts have arose (*sic*) in the Province touching the authority of the present Chief Baron, we conceive it is not advisable to rest the authority of erecting such Court and appointing the Chief Baron on the present Commission and Instructions; but yet it would be more proper (if His Majesty should be so pleased), by a Special Commission to his Governor, to authorize the establishment of such a Court, and the constitution of the Chief Baron and other officers of it."

Attorney-General Sir D. Ryder, on March 27, 1750, gave an opinion to the effect, that the King could not grant power to establish a Criminal Court in Newfoundland, except under the Great Seal.† He says: "I am of opinion such power cannot be granted by Instruction, or any otherwise than under the Great Seal; and, therefore, if thought advisable to be granted at all, ought to be inserted in the Governor's Commission; but the manner of his exercising such power may be prescribed and limited

---

* Forsyth, pp. 169-170.   † *Ibid.*, p. 172.

by Instructions, for any breach of which he will be answerable to His Majesty."

If a Queen's Counsel is an Officer of the Court, competent, on occasion, to adjudicate in criminal cases, the power to appoint him, ought, in accordance with the former of the opinions just cited, to be embodied in the Governor-General's Commission. In the appointment of Queen's Counsel in Canada, it must be borne in mind that the Royal prerogative, even supposing that it is legally exercised by the Governor-General, is, in the very nature of the case, limited and localized. A Queen's Counsel, appointed by the Governor-General, would have no *status*, as such, in any court in the British Islands. He cannot even take pre-audience or precedence in the Provincial Courts of Canada. But when the Queen, through the Governor-General, creates a Knight or a Baronet, the distinction is recognized in Great Britain, in Canada, in Australia, throughout the British Empire.

In the British North American Colonies, in the olden times, a Crown Counsel could not claim precedence on account of his title. In the "Rules of Precedency for the Settlement of the Precedency of Men and Women in America," a Crown Counsel was not even named.[*] According to these Rules "the members of the Assembly, Crown officers, &c., of any particular Province, have no other rank out of their Province than what belongs to them in their private capacity as men."

In England, where the title originated, it has never

---

[*] Stokes, p. 190.

been considered of sufficient importance to establish a claim to precedence outside of a court. Selden, in his Titles of Honour, does not mention it. Haydn's Book of Dignities,* ranks it after Serjeant-at-Law. "The Table of Precedence within the Dominion of Canada," ignores it.† Notwithstanding these instances of unrecognition, the title of Queen's Counsel, in Canada, is one that has long, and justly, been regarded as unmistakeable evidence of professional eminence and intellectual ability; one that has been, and still is worn by some of our most distinguished men.

But, as matters now stand, the Provincial authorities have the sole power to appoint Queen's Counsel. The Federal authorities, according to the reasonable and apparent interpretation of the Royal Commission, have no right to appoint Queen's Counsel; not even to give them pre-audience and precedence in the Supreme Court.

---

* Page 251.

† Mackintosh : Canadian Parliamentary Companion, 1879. Pages 100-101.

CHAPTER XXI.

ARE THE PROVINCES REPUBLICS?

IN the Canada *Law Journal*, of December, 1879, will be found a report of the decision of the Supreme Court in Lenoir *et al.*, appellants, and Ritchie, respondent: the Great Seal case.

In this decision one of the learned Judges is made to say:

Dictum—" The Provincial Governments are, as it were, carved out of, and subordinated to, the Dominion."

Answer—" Whereas the Provinces of Canada, Nova Scotia and New Brunswick have expressed their desire to be federally united into one Dominion, under the Crown of the Kingdom of Great Britain and Ireland," etc. (Preamble B. N. A. Act.)

Dictum—" The Queen forms no part of the Provincial Legislatures, as she does of the Dominion Parliament," etc.

Answer 1.—See concluding paragraph of preamble of the B. N. A. Act, cited above: " to be federally united into one Dominion, under the Crown of the United Kingdom," etc.

Answer 2.—"The Lieutenant-Governor of Ontario, and of Quebec shall, from time to time, in the Queen's name, by instrument under the Great Seal of the Province, summon and call together the Legislative Assembly of the Province." (B. N. A. Act, sec. 82.)

It is plain that when the Legislature is summoned in the Queen's name, she not only originates its existence, but that she is, throughout the whole term of that existence, a part of it; and a participant in all its acts and functions. It is worthy of particular observation that the very same language used in reference to the calling of the Provincial, is used in respect to the calling of the Federal Parliament. For example: " The Governor-General shall, from time to time, in the Queen's name, by instrument, under the Great Seal of Canada, summon and call together the House of Commons." (B. N. A. Act, sec. 38.)

It is also to be carefully noticed that, by the 82nd section, the Lieutenant-Governor, as respects the greatest of all the functions of a Colonial Viceroy, that of summoning Parliament, is empowered to act as the direct representative of Her Majesty. In this one duty he stands on the same level with the Governor-General himself. In other words, the Queen, through the Lieutenant-Governor, becomes a vital and visible participant in the legislation of the Provincial Parliaments.

Answer 3.—" . . . . The Lieutenant-Governors of the Canadian Provinces are expressly named in the Queen's Commission appointing the Governor-General, and are therein empowered ' to exercise, from time to time, as they may judge necessary, all powers lawfully belonging' to the Sovereign, ' in respect of assembling or proroguing, and of dissolving, the Legislative Councils, or the Legislative or General Assemblies, of those Provinces respectively.'" This answer is taken from a pamphlet entitled "A Constitutional Governor."* The author, Mr. Alpheus Todd, the Librarian of the Federal Parliament, is one of the greatest living masters and exponents of the principles of Parliamentary and Constitutional Government.

Answer 4.—(From the Earl of Dufferin's Commission, 22 May, 1872.†) "And we do further authorize and empower you to exercise, from time to time, as you may judge necessary, all powers lawfully belonging to Us, in respect of assembling or proroguing the Senate or the House of Commons of Our said Dominion, and of dissolving the said House of Commons, and we do hereby give the like authority to the several Lieutenant-Governors for the time being, of the Provinces in Our said Dominion, with respect to the Legislative Councils or the Legislative or General Assemblies of those Provinces respectively."

Dictum.—" The Queen is no party to the laws made by these Local Legislatures."

Answer 1.—" He (the Sovereign) is also the head of the Imperial Legislature, which derives its existence from the Crown, and a component part of every Local Legislature throughout his Dominions." ‡

Answer 2.—" Moreover, in all the British Colonies,

---
* Pp. 29-30.   † Journals of Canada, 1873, p. 89.
‡ Todd: Parliamentary Government in England, vol. 1, p. 167.

every act of the Executive runs in the name of the Queen. Parliaments, whether Federal or Provincial, are opened in her name and by her Governors. 'Legislation,' says Mr. Disraeli, 'is carried on in her name—even in Provinces, as in Canada, which are directly subordinate to a Federal Government, instead of to Imperial authority.' . . . . 'So that, in a modified, but most real sense, even the Lieutenant-Governors of the Canadian Provinces are representatives of the Crown."*

Dictum: "No Act of any such Legislatures (Local), can in any manner impair or affect Her Majesty's right to the exclusive exercise of all her prerogative power."

Answer 1.—See, on page 97, Hon. Attorney-General Mowat's argument as to prerogative, in the matter of Escheats. See, also, on page 109, the decision of the five Judges of the Court of Queen's Bench in Quebec, sitting in Appeal.

Answer 2.—"In all these Colonies† the Imperial Government retains only the appointment of the Governor, and a veto on legislation—(which privileges, in the case of the Provinces in the Canadian Dominion, are now exercised by the Governor-General in Council)—and has no con-control over any public functionary except the Governor."

"To the same effect, we are reminded by the Duke of Argyle, that the nomination of Governors is almost the sole remaining bond of connection between the Mother

---

* "A Constitutional Governor," p. 30.

† The Canadian Provinces, the five Provinces of Australia, New Zealand, Tasmania, and the Cape of Good Hope. "A Constitutional Governor," p. 12.

country and Colonies possessing Parliamentary Institutions."*

Answer 3.—The Crown has long ago abandoned the exercise of practical prerogative in Canada. The power, without responsible Ministerial advice, to create Judges, and then to give them permanent seats in the Legislature, has been surrendered. The power to nominate Bishops of the Anglican church has been given up. Further than this, the Royal Prerogative, in one of its most vital attributes, the power to enforce the decisions of the Courts, has been waived in respect to Canada. For Lord Monk, in his Speech, at the opening of Parliament, on the 21st of March, 1862,† informed the Legislature that a Bill was about to be introduced into the Imperial Parliament, to abolish the power of the Superior Courts in England to issue the writ of *Habeas Corpus* into this and other Colonies.

Answer 4. The Queen being eliminated from Provincial Legislation, the " Provinces of Canada, Nova Scotia and New Brunswick " are not " under the Crown of Great Britain and Ireland;" they must then be independent Republics.

---

* "A Constitutional Governor," p. 32. See also Report Hon. W. E. Gladstone's Remarks, p. 53.

† Journals, 1862. Imperial Act, 25-26 Vic., Cap. 20.

CHAPTER XXII.

THE QUEEN'S NAME IN PROVINCIAL LEGISLATION.

THERE are those who advance the theory that the Provincial Parliaments of Canada have no legal right to use the name of the Queen in their legislation. It has been already shown in these pages that the Queen is a participant in the law-making functions of these Parliaments. It now remains to prove that even if the name of Her Majesty were left out of the enacting part of the Acts of the Canadian Provincial Legislatures, the omission would not, according to precedent, invalidate the laws that are made.

The precedents, in this case, is the practice in the Legislatures of the Thirteen Colonies, when they were still members of the British Empire. We shall reproduce the enacting part of the Acts of the more important of these Colonies.

The enacting part of an Act of Assembly in Virginia before the Civil War:—

"Be it therefore enacted, by the Lieutenant-Governor, Council, and Burgesses, of this present General Assembly, and it is hereby enacted by the authority of the same, that, etc."*

The enacting part of an Act of Assembly of the Province of the Massachusetts Bay, before the Civil War:—

---

* Stokes, pp. 246-247.

"Be it enacted by His Excellency the Governor, Council, and Representatives, in General Court assembled, and by the authority of the same, that, etc."*

The enacting part of an Act of Assembly of the Province of New York, before the Civil War:—

"Be it therefore enacted by the Governor, Council, and General Assembly, and by the authority of the same, that, etc."†

The enacting part of an Act of Assembly in the Province of Georgia, before the Civil War:—

"We humbly pray His most Sacred Majesty that it may be enacted, and be it enacted by His Excellency, . . . Captain-General and Governor-in-Chief in and over His Majesty's Province of Georgia, by and with the advice and consent of the Honourable Council, and the Commons House of Assembly of the said Province, in General Assembly met, and by the authority of the same, that, etc."‡

It will be observed that there is the most striking dissimilarity in the enacting part of the Acts in the Province of Virginia, and in the Province of Georgia. In the former case the name of the King is completely ignored. An Act of Virginia would not show, of itself, that the King of Great Britain was the head of the Colony, or that he took any part in the enactment of the laws. On the other hand, the enacting part of an Act of the Province of Georgia is remarkable for the prominence which it gives to the King, and for the phraseology in which he is men-

---
* Stokes, p. 247. † *Ibid.*, p. 248. ‡ *Ibid.*, pp. 248-249.

tioned. But, notwithstanding this glaring difference between the enacting parts of the Acts of Virginia and Georgia, the validity of their respective Statutes was in every case the same.

The Imperial authorities, in those older times, did not carp and quibble over the phraseology of an Act of the Colonial Assemblies. They did not insist that Virginia, and Massachusetts Bay, and New York should follow the example of the Province of Georgia. They considered that, as long as the Colonies recognized the joint Sovereignty of the King and the British Parliament, they were free, as self-governed communities, to enact laws in whatever language seemed to them most suitable. The Home authorities did not cease to recognize the Constitutional force of the opinion of Attorney-General Raymond, on an Act of Assembly of Barbadoes, passed on August 1, 1712, which was :—

"That an Act of Assembly has the same effect in the Colonies, as an Act of Parliament has in the Mother Country."*

The enacting part of an Act of the Dominion of Canada is :—

Her Majesty, by and with the advice and consent of the Senate and House of Commons of Canada, enacts as follows :—

The enacting part of an Act of the Province of Ontario :—

Her Majesty, by and with the advice and consent of

---

* Chalmers' Colonial opinions, p. 351.

the Legislative Assembly of the Province of Ontario, enacts as follows :—

The enacting part of an Act of the Province of Quebec :—

Her Majesty, by and with the advice and consent of the Legislature of Quebec, enacts as follows :—

Now, if the words "Her Majesty" were eliminated from the enacting part of the Acts of Ontario and Quebec, there would be no greater difference between those enacting parts so modified, and the enacting part of an Act of the Federal Parliament, than there was in the phraseology of the Virginia and Georgia Statutes. The opinion of Attorney-General Raymond would still hold good. The Legislatures of Ontario and Quebec, could continue to enact, within the powers prescribed by the B. N. A. Act, laws that would have "the same effect in the Colonies as an Act of Parliament has in the Mother Country."

CHAPTER XXIII.

THE STRUGGLE AND TRIUMPH OF THE LEGISLATURE OF JAMAICA.

IN the Constitutional Annals of the British Colonies, there is, probably, no more instructive story than that of the struggle and triumph of the Legislature of Jamaica. On the one side, was the House of Assembly, battling for its privileges: on the other, were ranged Major-General Carmichael, the Commander of Forces, and his ally, the Duke of Manchester, the Governor of the Island.

The incidents of this remarkable contest are now, it is believed for the first time, brought forth from the obscurity of official documents into the light of publicity.* They are as follow—

In the House of Assembly, in Jamaica, on 1st November, 1808, a Committee was appointed to make inquiry as to the circumstances of the late mutiny in the 2nd West India Regiment, at Fort Augusta ; and to report the facts, with their opinions thereon, to the House. The Committee was to have power to send for persons, papers and records ; and to examine all persons that should come before them.

On the 2nd of November, the Chairman of the Committee reported its recommendation to the House: namely, to send a message to the Duke of Manchester, the Governor of the Island, requesting him to cause to be laid before the House authenticated copies of all proceedings taken before the Courts-Martial and Courts of Inquiry respecting the said mutiny.

On the 17th of November, the Speaker, Mr. Philip Redwood, by command of the Duke of Manchester, laid before the House the answer the Duke had received from Major-General Carmichael, Commander of the Forces, to a letter which his Grace addressed to him in consequence of the message of the House of the 2nd instant.

---

* Journals of the Honourable House of Assembly of Jamaica, 1808-1809.

The letter of Major-General Carmichael stated that he did not feel himself authorized or justifiable in delivering any authenticated copies of proceedings of general Courts-Martial.

The message of the House to the Duke of Manchester, and the letter of Major-General Carmichael, were referred to the Committe of the Whole House, appointed to inquire into and take into consideration the state of the Island.

This Committee reported a Resolution :—it was to request the Governor to cause the attendance of Captain Tonge and Major McLean, of the 2nd West India Regiment, for examination before a special Committee appointed to inquire into the mutiny in that corps, and the murder of two of his Majesty's officers of the same.

On the 29th of November, the Mutiny Committee reported to the Assembly that, in pursuance of the message of the House to the Governor, of the 22nd instant, they were attended by Captain Tonge and Major McLean. But the inquiry which they were directed to make, had been completely frustrated by a general order issued by Major-General Carmichael.

This order, which was dated the 25th of November, 1808, ran thus :—

"The Major-General feels it a paramount duty to apprise any officer, or other persons in a military capacity, that may be allowed to appear, that he does not permit them to answer any questions that the Legislative Body of this Island may put, upon the subject of a late mutiny, or upon the Government and discipline of His Majesty's forces."

The House unanimously agreed to the six resolutions which follow :—

Resolved, 1st. That this House, as the representatives of the people, hath of right and ever has exercised within the Island, all the powers, privileges and immunities claimed and enjoyed by the Commons House of Parliament, within the United Kingdom of Great Britain and Ireland.

Resolved, 2nd. That it is the undoubted privilege of the House to send for all papers and records, and to order the attendance of all persons, civil and military, resident within the Island, capable of giving evidence on any subject, under investigation in the House; that to prevent the attendance of witnesses, duly summoned, or pretend to prohibit such witnesses from giving full and true answers to all questions whatever, that may be propounded for discovering the truth, are breaches of the privileges of the House.

Resolved, 3rd. That requiring the attendance of the officers, non-commissioned officers and privates of His Majesty's forces on the House, to be ordered by the Governor or Lieutenant-Governor, who heretofore was commander of such forces, in place of bringing them by summons, has been matter of courtesy, in case they might, at the same time, have been ordered on other duty, and is not of right : and that the courtesy of the House has been uniformly returned by an immediate order for the attendance of all such persons, without any attempt to suppress the truth, or garble their testimony.

Resolved, 4th. That as the Grand Inquest of the country, it is the right and duty of the House to inquire into all grievances or matters which happen within the Island, dangerous to the public safety, . . . to the end that such representations may be made to our most gracious Sovereign, or such Legislative measures adopted as shall procure redress, etc.

Resolved, 5th. [This resolution set forth that, on the 27th of May, 1808, a mutiny broke out in the 2nd West India Regiment, when two of their officers were murdered, and many other persons were put to death. That no Coroner's inquest was held to inquire into the murders, or the causes by which the said other persons came to a violent death; that no investigation by the civil power, or trial of the murderers in the Courts of this Colony, had taken place. That the mutiny, &c., murders, and violent deaths had occasioned the greatest alarm to the inhabitants, who expected, on the meeting of their representatives, a full and impartial inquiry. The Resolution narrated the proceedings that had been taken by the House to procure information, referring particularly to the General Order from Major-General Carmichael, refusing permission to his officers to answer the questions of the Legislature.]

Resolved, 6th. That the assumption by Major-General Carmichael of a power to obstruct this House in the exercise of its rightful functions, inquiring into the causes of a mutiny which has excited the greatest alarm . . . by pretending to permit or prevent the attendance of witnesses, or prohibit them from answering any questions that by this House, or its Committees, may be thought necessary, and which do not criminate such witnesses, is an unconstitutional attempt to deprive this House of its undoubted rights, by an arbitrary exertion of military authority, and a gross violation of the most important privileges of the House.

The House further

Resolved, That Mr. Speaker do issue his warrant requiring the attendance of Major-General Carmichael at the Bar, on the 1st of December, to be examined touching a breach of the privileges of this House.

On November 30th, the Speaker informed the House that his Summons to Major-General Carmichael to attend at the Bar, pursuant to the Order of the House, had been personally served by the Deputy Messenger.

On the same day, November 30th, a Message from the Governor, by his Secretary, was read to the House.

" Mr. Speaker,—I am commanded by His Grace, the Governor, to lay before the House a copy of a letter he has just received from Major-General Carmichael ; and I am desired by His Grace to say that he perfectly agrees in the sentiments therein expressed. His Grace, considering the importance of the question as relative to the House, and also to the Major-General, as Commander of His Majesty's Forces in this Island, earnestly hopes that the House will give to any future proceedings upon it that serious consideration which the magnitude of the subject demands."

The letter of Major-General Carmichael, to the Duke of Manchester, bearing date November 30, 1808, informed His Grace that he, the General, had been, that morning served with an Order from the House of Assembly to appear at their Bar, next day, for the purpose of being examined touching a breach of privilege.

The letter proceeded:—" As I cannot acknowledge the authority of that Body, in a military point of view, over His Majesty's troops, ... I feel it my duty to wait the orders of H.R.H. the Commander-in-Chief, before I can submit to any jurisdiction or control the House of Assembly may attempt to assume over H.M. forces ; and without any intentional disrespect or contempt for that Honourable House in their Legislative capacity, I must decline attending according to their summons, as His Majesty's service requires my attendance at headquarters."

The Message was ordered to lie on the table, and the House forthwith adjourned.

On the 1st of December, the House again met, and the time appointed for Major-General Carmichael's appearance at the Bar being passed, and he not appearing, pursuant to Mr. Speaker's summons, it was

Resolved, nem. con. That Major-General Carmichael be taken into the custody of the Sergeant-at-Arms, for a contempt of this House, in not attending at the Bar this day, to be examined touching a breach of the privileges of the House; and that Mr. Speaker do issue his warrant accordingly.

The Governor's message, of the previous day, having been read, the House unanimously adopted the following resolutions :—

1. That it is the ancient and undoubted right and privilege of this House, that no notice ought to be taken by the other branches of the Legislature of any matter in agitation or debate in this House, but on information regularly communicated by this House to such other branch; and that, for the Governor of this Island to manifest or declare consent or dissent, approbation, or dislike, of any such matter, before it be presented to him, according to the order and course of Parliament, and of the Assembly of this Island, is a breach of the privileges of this House.

2. That the Message of His Grace, the Governor, of the 30th of November, accompanying a copy of a letter from Major-General Carmichael, communicating his intention to decline attending, agreeable to a Summons from this House, sitting as the Grand Inquest of the country, and declaring that His Grace perfectly agrees in the sentiments expressed in the said letter; and further taking notice of future proceedings that may be adopted on a question in agitation, acknowledged to be of importance to this House and the Major-General, is a breach of the privileges of this House.

3. That this House cannot, consistently with its own dignity, or with due regard to its rights and privileges,

which are the firmest bulwarks of the liberties, franchises and immunities of the people, proceed to any other business until reparation shall be made for the breach of its privileges.

Resolved, That a Message be sent to His Grace the Governor, with copies of the three Resolutions.

The same day a message came from the Governor, by the Provost Marshall, commanding, in the King's name, the immediate attendance of the whole House in the Council Chamber: whereupon, Mr. Speaker and the whole House went up.

The Governor then delivered the following speech :

"The House of Assembly having ordered the attendance of the Commander of H.M. Forces at their Bar, and intending, as it appears to me, to enforce that order, a measure certainly novel, and giving rise to a question of the greatest magnitude, as it tends, in fact, to devolve the command of any British army in this Island upon that House, I feel it incumbent upon me, however I lament any interruption to that harmony subsisting between the different branches of this Legislature, to take such measures as shall bring so important a point before the highest authority, previous to any further proceedings. The Governor then prorogued the Assembly until the 27th day of December next.

"The question remained in abeyance until the 25th of April, 1809, the first day of a new Session. The Governor, on that day, addressed the Speaker and the Assembly, as follows :

"Mr. Speaker and Gentlemen of the Assembly: I have it in command from His Majesty to acquaint you that he has been graciously pleased to direct a copy of the minutes of the Court-Martial to be laid before you, pursuant to your message of the 2nd of November last. . . . And I am also to acquaint you that the officers whose attendance you requested me to procure, by your message of the 22nd of Nov. last, will be directed to attend you, without being subjected to the restrictions contained in Major-General Carmichael's order of the 25th of November last.

"His Majesty entertains no doubt that you will adhere, in requiring such attendance in future, to those forms of proceeding which are sanctioned by precedent; and that you will direct your examination, on all occasions, in such manner as to avoid requiring from such officers disclosures, which, if made, might be attended with prejudice to the interests of His Majesty's service.

"I am desirous of assuring you that, so far from having any wish to interfere with, it has been my earnest desire to maintain and support, at all times, your accustomed rights and privileges; confident, in so doing, I shall promote the interests of the Island, and fulfil the gracious intentions of His Majesty."

The entries in the Journals of the 29th and 30th of November, and 1st of December, of last Session, respecting the mutiny, etc., so far as related to Major-General Carmichael, having been read, it was:

Resolved, nem. con., That Mr. Speaker, *pro tempore*, do issue his Warrant for taking into custody Major-General Carmichael, who was ordered into custody during the last Session on a Resolution of the House, that he had violated its privileges, and for a contempt of the House in not attending on Mr. Speaker's Summons, to be examined touching the said breach of privileges.

On the 26th of April, 1809, Major-General Carmichael, attending at the Bar, in the custody of the Serjeant-at-Arms, was asked by the Speaker, *pro tempore*, what he had to say for himself in respect to the two breaches of privilege—the issuing of the General Order, and the refusal to attend the summons of the House to be examined touching that Order.

Major-General Carmichael said: "My high sense of military duty induced me to await the orders of my Sovereign previous to attending your summons. I regret that this measure should have been deemed a breach of the privileges of this House—never in my contemplation. I am now ready to attend the pleasure of this honourable House, *having received His Majesty's commands for so doing.*" (The italics are own own.)

Ordered that Major-General Carmichael be discharged.

Resolved, That His Grace, the Governor, having in his Speech, at the opening of the Session, been graciously pleased to assure the House that, so far from having any wish to interfere with, it has been his earnest desire to maintain and support, at all times, the accustomed rights and privileges of the House, the House is satisfied that the Message of the 30th November last was without any intention of violating the privileges of the House.

On the 27th of April, an Address was ordered to be presented to the Governor. It contains the following, amongst other paragraphs :

" Every right and privilege exercised by the Commons House of Parliament within the United Kingdom of Great Britain and Ireland, being inherent in the representatives of the people of this Island, met in General Assembly, we cannot receive as a favour, depending on the direction of His Majesty's Government, the attendance of witnesses required by the House ; nor can we recognize its authority to remove the unconstitutional restrictions attempted to be imposed by Major-General Carmichael's order of the 25th of November last, which supposes the power of continuing such restrictions, or renewing them, when deemed expedient.

"We beg leave to observe that the House has at all times regulated its proceedings by Constitutional principles and established procedents ; and your Grace may confidently assure His Majesty's Government that, in ordering the attendance of witnesses, and conducting their examinations, we shall strictly adhere to the regular usage of Parliament.

"We received with the highest satisfaction your Grace's assurances of an earnest desire to maintain and support at all times our accustomed rights and privileges in place of entertaining a wish to interfere with them. . . .

On the same day, the 27th of April, the Governor laid

before the House the proceedings of a general Court Martial, held at Jamaica, May 30th, 1808, and on subsequent days. And thus the House triumphed in the Constitutional struggle with a military commander, who, in his own sphere was practically an autocrat, and with a Governor who, as the King's Representative, but, as the event proved, without the King's sanction, lent to the autocrat the aid and sanction of his exalted office.

The action of the Jamaica House of Assembly, in vindication of its own privileges, and in upholding the rights of those whom it represented, adds an honoured page to the history of the Constitutional struggles and victories of Colonial Legislatures.

CHAPTER XXIV.

THE MAGNA CHARTA OF THE BRITISH COLONIES.

LORD ABINGDON stated in the debate in the House of Lords, on the Constitutional Act of 1791 :*

". . . That by this Bill this country was restored to its right, *not of internal legislation over the Colonies, for that right it never had,* notwithstanding the pretended omnipotence of the Declaratory Act,† but to its undoubted external right of regulating the commerce of all its De-

---

* Hansard's Parliamentary History, vol. 29, pp. 658-659.
† 18, Geo. 3, cap. 12.

pendencies, for the sake of the navigation, and, insomuch, for the safety and general benefit of the whole British Empire."

The Declaratory Act was 18, Geo. 3, cap. 12. The authority of the Imperial Parliament to impose internal taxation on the Thirteen Colonies was asserted by a previous Act 6, Geo. 3, cap. 12. It was the attempt to exercise this power which led to the loss of the American Colonies. All too late came the Declaratory Act, which essayed to undo the deplorable effects of the Act 6, Geo. 3, cap. 12.

The Declaratory Act recites :—

" That taxation by the Parliament of Great Britain, for the purpose of raising a revenue in His Majesty's Colonies, Provinces, and Plantations in North America, has been found, by experience, to produce great uneasiness and disorders among His Majesty's faithful subjects, who may, nevertheless, be disposed to acknowledge the justice of contributing to the common defence of the Empire, provided such contribution should be raised under the authority of the General Court or General Assembly of each respective Colony, Province or Plantation.

" And whereas, in order as well to remove the said uneasiness, etc., it is expedient to declare, that the King and Parliament of Great Britain will not impose any duty, tax, or assessment, for the purpose of raising a revenue, in any of the Colonies, Provinces and Plantations."

" From and after the passing of this Act, the King and Parliament of Great Britain will not impose any duty, tax, or assessment whatever, payable in any of His Majesty's Colonies, Provinces or Plantations in North America or the West Indies, except only such duties as it may be expedient to impose for the regulation of commerce; the net produce of such duties to be always paid and applied to and for the use of the Colony, Province, or Plantation, in which the same shall be respectively levied, in such manner as other duties, collected by the authority of the respective General Courts, or General Assemblies of such Colonies, Provinces, or Plantations, are ordinarily paid and applied."

This Declaratory Act may well be regarded as the Magna Charta of every British Colony possessing Representative Institutions.

CHAPTER XXV.

THE DANGERS OF FEDERAL CENTRALIZATION.

IT is the solemn duty of each of the British North American Provinces keenly to watch, and promptly to repel, any attempt, faint or forcible, which the Federal Government or a Federal Court might be disposed to make on the rights and privileges of the Members of the Confederation.

The history of the Federal idea, on this Continent, is fraught with important warnings. Its great aim, in the

United States, has been, since the infancy of the Constitution, to become strong at the expense of the separate Sovereignties, which were the original sources of Federal existence. The words Federal authority and centralization have become, on the Southern side of our frontier, almost equivalent expressions. But States Rights and Provincial Rights are the strongest bulwarks against despotism. In a Federation, diversity is freedom; uniformity is bondage.

It is only weak minds, and men cast in a servile mould, who cry out for strong governments. The political or social sybarite, shrinking from the performance of the ennobling duties of free citizenship, and afraid of its manly struggles, longs for the dishonourable ease and personal irresponsiblity of a despotism. Such a despotism can be found in a Federal Government, as well as in the rule of an autocrat. Under whatever form or name it may be exercised, the power which is unquestioned and unchallenged, is but another name for tyranny.

THE END.

APPENDICES.

APPENDIX No. 1.

DEFINITION OF "LEGISLATURE."

Legislature.—The power that makes laws.—(Johnson's Dictionary.)

"In the notion of a Legislature is implied a power to change, repeal, and suspend laws in being, as well as to make new laws."—(Addison, quoted by Johnson.)

Legislature.—The body of persons in a state or kingdom, invested with power to make and repeal laws; the supreme power of a State.—(Craig's English Dictionary.) In Webster, edition of 1874, there is precisely the same definition.

Legislative.—Making, giving or enacting laws; as a Legislative Body or Assembly. Relating, or pertaining to the passing of laws; suitable to laws.—(Zell's Encyclopedia.)

Legislature.— The power that makes laws.— (Wharton's Law Lexicon.)

Legislature.—That body of men in the State which has the power of making laws.—(Bouvier's Law Dictionary.)

Legislature.—The body in a State invested with the power of making or repealing laws; the supreme power in a State.—(Stormonth.)

"The terms 'Legislature' and 'Colonial Legislature' shall severally signify the authority, other than the Imperial Parliament or Her Majesty in Council, competent to make laws for any colony." —[Preamble to 28 and 29 Vic., cap. 63 (Imperial Act.)]

APPENDIX No. 2.

EXPENDITURE FOR CIVIL GOVERNMENT IN ONTARIO AND CANADA.

"The people of this Province have been taught by the practical lessons of the period from 1841 to 1867, how specially important it is to their welfare and good government that such public matters as the management and sale of the public lands and the revenues therefrom, as well as from mines and minerals, the control of our municipal institutions, supreme authority over property and civil rights, the efficient administration of justice, and the responsibility of educating the whole people of the Province, should be regulated by a Legislature conversant with such subjects, and their bearings upon the interests of the Province. . . . . .

"The one colourable argument for such a step, (Legislative Union), is the assumed expense of carrying on the two systems of Government; but if the expenditure of the Province of Ontario for the purpose of Legislation (which is one of the few subjects which could be dispensed with), amounting to $111,250 and a portion under Civil Government saved, the total economy effected for the year 1879 would amount to about the sum of $150,000; for the expenditure for all other Provincial objects would be as necessary under a Legislative Union as now, and with the certain danger of larger amounts being required owing to the difficulty of managing as economically at Ottawa as at Toronto; and if this argument of expense is to be pressed, a simpler mode of diminishing the general expenditure would be in the reduction, which could readily be made without detriment to the efficiency of the public service or to Canadian interests, in the expense of Civil Government and Legislation at Ottawa.—(Hon. Adam Crooks, Minister of Education, pamphlet "Reform Government in Ontario," pp. 9-10., 1879.)

APPENDIX No. 3.

THE COLONIAL SECRETARY PRONOUNCES AGAINST A COURT OF APPEAL.

Sir John Young, on the 11th of March, 1869, in a despatch to the Earl of Granville, Secretary of State, for the Colonies says amongst other matters : *

"It is worthy of consideration whether it would not be expedient

---

* S. P. C. 1870, No. 35, pp. 3-5.

to establish a tribunal with powers analogous to those of the Supreme Court of the United States, for the decision of all questions of Constitutional Law and conflict of jurisdiction.

"The British North America Act (sec. 101), empowers the Parliament of Canada to establish a General Court of Appeal; but I am advised that Imperial Legislation will be required to enable the Dominion Parliament to establish a Court with original jurisdiction over such subjects.

"The organization of a Court of Appeal is, I am told, likely to engage the attention of the Parliament here at the coming Session, and that then the whole subject of the best means of determining these respective jurisdictions, and of settling Constitutional questions generally, will probably be discussed in all its bearings. I propose, in such case, to address you again on the subject."

To this Earl Granville replies, in a despatch dated Downing Street, 8th May, 1869:

"With regard to your remark, that it is worthy of consideration, whether it would not be expedient to establish a tribunal for the decision of all questions of Constitutional Law and conflict of jurisdiction, I see no reason for the establishment of such a tribunal. Any question of this kind could be entertained and decided by the Local Courts, subject to an appeal to the Judicial Committee of the Privy Council, and it does not appear in what respect this mode of determination is likely to be inadequate or unsatisfactory.

"I have, etc.,

"GRANVILLE."

APPENDIX No. 4.

THE LOCAL LEGISLATURE.

"If our form of government cannot stand the fullest and freest discussion of every subject in the realm of politics, then are we not free men, and the much vaunted liberty of the subject is a farce.

"The Local system has been in existence only twelve years, and during that time it has, on the whole, worked well. The Legislature has devoted much attention to the development of the country, and the result is visible in the increase of population, the wonderful growth of railroad enterprises, and the steady march of civilization northward towards the Height of Land. The educational interests of the people have also been carefully attended to; the three R's have been brought to every man's door, and higher education is within easy reach of the poorest. This inestimable boon has not been secured without a lavish expenditure, but money invested in schools is bread cast upon the waters. No one, we think, will begrudge the Legislature its due meed of praise for dealing in a generous and intelligent spirit with education and colonization, which, after all, are the paramount questions in a new country.

. . . . . Certainly, it will not be contended that the business of the Province would have been transacted as well, or more cheaply, by a Legislative Union. The bitter experiences of the political vendetta that rent Upper and Lower Canada, and made the Union of 1841 a grim satire on unity, ought to satisfy every thinking man that such a form of government is not suited for a country of mixed races. It is tolerably certain, indeed, that if one Parliament had to deal with the local as well as the general interests of the seven Provinces, the work would be badly done, if done at all, and the sectionalism that now curses us would become an intolerable drag on progress and a perpetual danger to the State.

"For good or evil, partyism enters into almost every branch of public life, and the only safe way of conducting public affairs that has yet suggested, itself is the old fashioned Legislature with the Outs watching the Ins, and the Ins kept on their best behaviour by the vigilance of the Outs. In the meantime it is better to stick to the tried methods with all their defects, than venture on risky Constitutional experiments, the failure of which would entail endless confusion and expense."—(Abridged from the *Mail*, January 6, 1880.)

www.ingramcontent.com/pod-product-compliance
Lightning Source LLC
Chambersburg PA
CBHW030300170426
43202CB00009B/815